ASPECTS OF BUILDINGS & MONUMENTS:
BRANXTON, CROOKHAM, ETAL, FORD

Also by Antony Chessell

The Life and Times of Abraham Hayward, Q.C., Victorian Essayist 'One of the two best read men in England', Lulu Publishing, 2009

A Small Share in the Conflict; The Wartime Diaries and Selected Correspondence of Flt Lt Henry Chessell (R.A.F. Intelligence Branch), edited by Antony Chessell, Lulu Publishing, 2009,

Coldstream Building Snippets   Cans, Quoins and Coursers, Lulu Publishing, 2010

The Braw Trees of Coldstream, Lulu Publishing, 2011

Leet Water: From Source to Tweed, Lulu Publishing, 2012

Breamish & Till: From Source to Tweed, TillVAS, 2014

Also by Gwen Chessell

Richard Spencer: Napoleonic Naval War Hero and Australian Pioneer, University of Western Australia Press, 2005

Alexander Collie: Colonial Surgeon, Naturalist and Explorer, University of Western Australia Press, 2008

Separate Lives: The Story of Sir George and Lady Grey, Hopping Mouse Press, 2014

Aspects of Buildings & Monuments:
Branxton, Crookham, Etal, Ford

Antony Chessell & Gwen Chessell

Foreword by Rt. Hon. Lord Joicey

Published by TillVAS

Published in 2019

Till Valley Archaeological Society (TillVAS),
Northumberland www.tillvas.com

Copyright © Antony Chessell & Gwen Chessell 2019

Antony Chessell & Gwen Chessell assert their moral right to be identified
as the authors of this work

A catalogue record for this book is available from the British Library

ISBN 978-0-244-75069-5

Typeset in Times New Roman

Printed and bound in Great Britain

Front cover: 13th to 20th century sandstone masonry at the Church of St. Michael
and All Angels, Ford

Cover design and photograph by the authors

All rights reserved. No part of this publication may be reproduced, stored in a private retrieval system, or transmitted in any form or by any means, electronic, mechanical, photocopying, recording or otherwise, without the prior permission of the authors

To the people of the four villages, the hamlets and the farms
Past, Present and Future

↑N

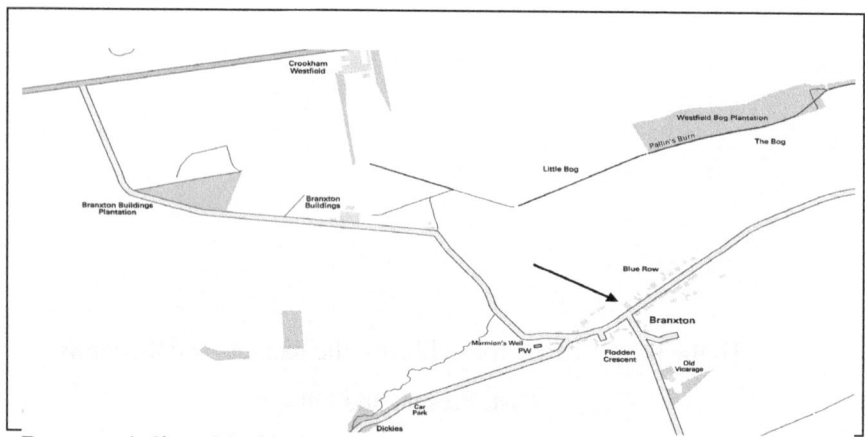

Branxton, indicated by black arrow, is situated to the west of Crookham, Etal and Ford. The A697 road from Cornhill-on-Tweed to Wooler runs left to right past Crookham Westfield at the top of the map. Contains Ordnance Survey data © Crown copyright and database rights 2019.

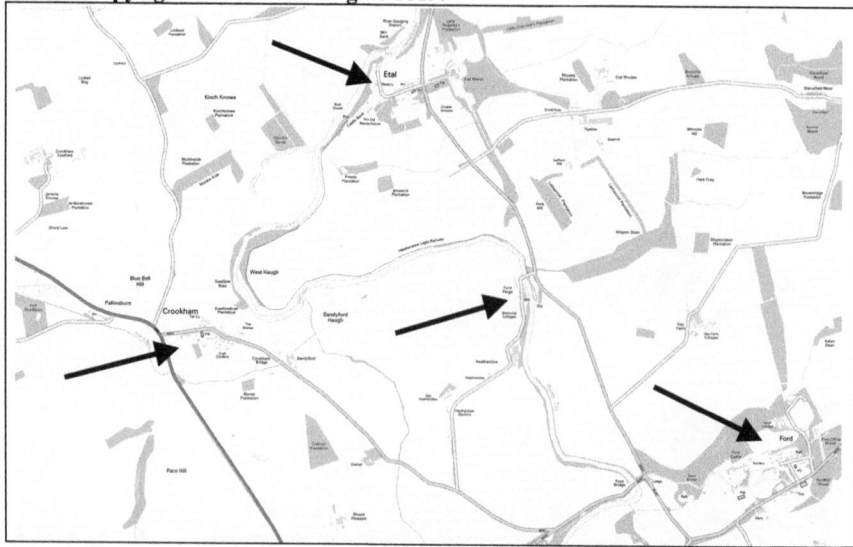

The A697 road runs from north-west to south-east past Crookham towards Wooler which is seven miles away as the crow flies. Crookham, Etal and Ford are indicated by black arrows, Also shown is the hamlet of Heatherslaw (Ford Forge). Contains Ordnance Survey data © Crown copyright and database rights 2019.

Contents

	Page
Illustrations, Access & Further Reading	viii
Acknowledgments	ix
Foreword	x
Introduction	xi
1. Geology and Building Stone	1
2. Building Styles	10
3. Wall Construction	48
4. Doors and Windows	71
5. Roofs	96
6. Bits and Pieces	130
7. Monuments and Memorials	155
Notes	189
Geology Appendix	193
Glossary of Building & Other Terms	198
Index	207

Illustrations

The illustrations have not been listed in a separate table and they just appear within the text with accompanying captions or explanations. However, they are referenced in the index. All images are from the authors' collection except where otherwise stated.

Access

The authors stress that they have not trespassed on any private property. Most of the building features are visible from roads, footpaths or other land with public access but whenever it was necessary to go on to private land, the owners and/or tenants have granted us permission.

Further Reading

There is no separate Bibliography other than the sources contained within the Notes. Readers may be interested in the following useful guides to the vocabulary, grammar and heritage of British buildings.

Rice's Architectural Primer, Matthew Rice, Bloomsbury Publishing Plc, 2009; *Village Buildings of Britain*, Matthew Rice, Time Warner Books UK, 2003; *Tracing the History of Houses*, Bill Breckon & Jeffrey Parker, Countryside Books, 2000; *Discovering Cottage Architecture*, Christopher Powell, Shire Publications Ltd., 1996.

Acknowledgments

We wish to thank Lord Joicey for kindly agreeing to write the foreword to this book. Lord Joicey takes a keen interest in local history and archaeology; he is Patron of our publishers, the Till Valley Archaeological Society (TillVAS) and is a Director of the Flodden 1513 Ecomuseum project. That project commemorated the 500th Anniversary of the battle and created the Flodden 500 project which left a lasting legacy of 41 Flodden related sites throughout England and Scotland.

We also thank the residents of the four villages and those who live in the countryside around them. They include the major landowners, Lord and Lady Joicey, Ford & Etal Estates, and Mr and Mrs George Farr, Pallinsburn Estate and the many house owners, tenants and farmers in the area. We have written this book for them because it is their and their predecessors' buildings and monuments that have furnished us with such rich material in this attractive and historic landscape of north Northumberland. Thanks are also due to members of the Historic Buildings Group of the Branxton & Crookham Village Atlas Project who provided the 'trigger' for this book.

We are grateful to our publishers for agreeing to publish the book and for giving us free rein to write a subjective account. All statements in the book remain our responsibility and are not put forward as the views of TillVAS. Any errors are our own.

Foreword

Rt. Hon. Lord Joicey, Ford & Etal Estates

It is often claimed that the built heritage of the United Kingdom attracts more interest and more visitors than in any other country. Organisations such as the National Trust, English Heritage, Historic Scotland or the Historic Houses Association maintain buildings of every description that tell important stories from our past yet are frequently still very much alive and thriving. The many 'period drama' series created for television or film, many of which are set in and around our castles, halls, manor houses and parkland, are immensely popular the world over.

One cannot deny that these famous and beautiful buildings are spectacular. But there is another and even more fascinating element of our built heritage, much more numerous and ubiquitous, usually referred to under the heading of 'vernacular architecture'. These are the humbler dwellings and constructions, seen in every village and in every community across the land. Some of them are extraordinarily old but still sound and viable. Their story is just as, if not more, important than the smarter and grander buildings that we are encouraged to visit. They tell us about local ways, local traditions and local craftsmen, the backbone of the British countryside.

Antony and Gwen Chessell have undertaken a remarkable study of the buildings of five small communities in the Till Valley of North Northumberland. Through scholarship and careful observation they illustrate and explain them, deftly yet thoroughly, helping to unpick the extraordinarily rich and complex history of this Border area in which folk have lived for many centuries.

This book will, I hope, encourage others to look at the villages and places where they themselves live, to see very familiar buildings, even the humblest, in a new light and to think about the history of building and craftsmanship that has led to the present-day character of their own community, for surely it is in the 'vernacular' where the true roots of the United Kingdom's built heritage lie.

James Joicey
January 2019

Introduction

Present and previous generations of our families have sketched, painted, and jotted things down in notebooks when 'pottering' around streets, buildings and churchyards throughout Britain, often with their heads in the air and sometimes a danger to themselves and to others. It is amazing what can be discovered; many of us give buildings only a glance as we pass, but it is worth stopping and taking time to examine details of their construction and embellishment.

This was our reasoning for writing the book but it was given added impetus by a working paper, *Building Materials and Features to be seen in Branxton and Crookham* that we produced during research carried out for the community-based Branxton & Crookham Village Atlas project that was administered by the Till Valley Archaeological Society (TillVAS). This was the starting point for the present book but we decided to widen the scope to include the two other villages that are so closely linked with Branxton and Crookham—the villages of Etal and Ford, as well as the hamlet of Heatherslaw. All four villages are completely different in appearance but they have historic bonds that create an entity well recognised by the present-day residents who share a community newsletter, *The Fourum* (sic). An important link between the communities is that large parts of the four villages and the hamlet fall within the two historic estates of Ford & Etal and Pallinsburn. We decided very early on not to focus on the history of individual and prominent buildings such as St. Paul's Church at Branxton, Etal Castle,

Ford Castle, St. Michael and All Angels Church, Ford and Pallinsburn House. Information is available elsewhere and we have only made historical reference to these and other buildings where appropriate when commenting on their building features or monuments.

Allen Mawer gives the origin of *Branxton* as being possibly from the Old English (OE) name, *Brannoc*, perhaps being a diminutive of *Brand* which may have a Norse origin. Godfrey Watson goes along with *Brannoc*, meaning 'Little Brand'. Also A. D. Mills suggests its meaning as being 'Farmstead of a man called Branoc', a Celtic person's name plus OE *tūn*.

Mawer says that *Crookham* is from Old West Scandinavian *krókr*, a crook or bend in a river and the Old English *ham* meaning village. Watson agrees with this and so does Mills.

Ford is self-explanatory and Mawer believes that *Etal*, *Ethale* or *Hethal* may originate from 'Haugh of Eata' with *Eata* being an Old Northumbrian name. Watson gives the origin as the 'Low Ground settled by Eata' and Mills gives the definition as a 'nook of land used for grazing' from the OE *ete* plus *halh*.

Mawer suggests that *Heatherslaw* may derive from *Hæðhere's Hill*. Whereas Watson agrees with this in relation to a Heatherslaw near Stamfordham (11 miles west of Newcastle), he suggests that 'our' Heatherslaw derives from a 'Hill frequented by Harts, that is to say, Stags'. Heatherslaw is not mentioned by Mills.

1
Geology and Building Stone

The underlying bedrock beneath the villages of Branxton, Crookham, Etal and Ford dates from the Carboniferous period when the sedimentary rocks of sandstone, siltstone and limestone sediments of various degrees of hardness were laid down in layers in shallow seas and lagoons, some 350 million years ago. Some of this geological area lies within what is known as the Ballagan Formation, so named after the Ballagan Glen north of Glasgow, and which continues into Northumberland. This area is shown marked 'C' on the map and key on pages 3 and 4.

To the east of the Ballagan Formation, the bedrocks comprise, firstly, the Fell Sandstone Formation (marked 'D') which is a friable, medium-grained sandstone and, secondly, the Tyne Limestone Formation (marked 'E') which tends to lie below other formations and contains coal seams. The igneous, plutonic outcrops (marked 'K') of the Great Whin Sill are very obvious features that extend in a high, semi-continuous ridge from Fenwick and Bamburgh and then down through south-central Northumberland. These outcrops of dolerite (see below) were intruded into the surrounding sandstone formation towards the end of the Carboniferous period.

To the west of the Ballagan Formation is the Cheviot Massif, the Cheviot Volcanic Formation (marked 'B'), which was formed from molten rock during the Devonian period, over 400 million years ago.

These are very hard, igneous rocks formed from extruded andesitic lava or magma into which were intruded granites of the central Cheviot Granite Pluton (marked 'A' and named after Pluto, the classical god of the underworld), and the radiating dykes of the Cheviot Dyke-swarm (marked 'N'). Many of these are reddish in colour when weathered, compared with the grey or blue of the adjoining volcanic rocks. Whereas extruded igneous rocks have erupted from volcanoes (eg. andesite, basalt) and spread on to the surface of the Earth, intruded igneous rocks originally cooled beneath the Earth's surface (eg. granite, gabbro, dolerite). The Cheviot Granite Pluton is on or close to the line of the Iapetus Suture which marks the point of collision (and the closure of the Iapetus Ocean) some 500 million years ago between the ancient continent of Laurentia which contained what is now Scotland and that of Avalonia containing what is now England.

These underlying bedrocks, whether sedimentary or igneous, have been overlaid in many places by material from the Quaternary period, the most recent of the 2.6 million years of Earth's history when glaciers and ice-sheets advanced from the Poles and then retreated, carving the land with each movement. In the northern hemisphere, these glaciers and ice-sheets covered the whole of northern Europe. In Britain, they probably reached as far down as the River Thames with the glacial flow carving out 'U'-shaped valleys, eroding mountains and depositing rocks, sand and gravel along the direction of travel. Material visible today is probably left over from the end of the last Ice Age, about 11,000 years ago.

Geology and Building Stone

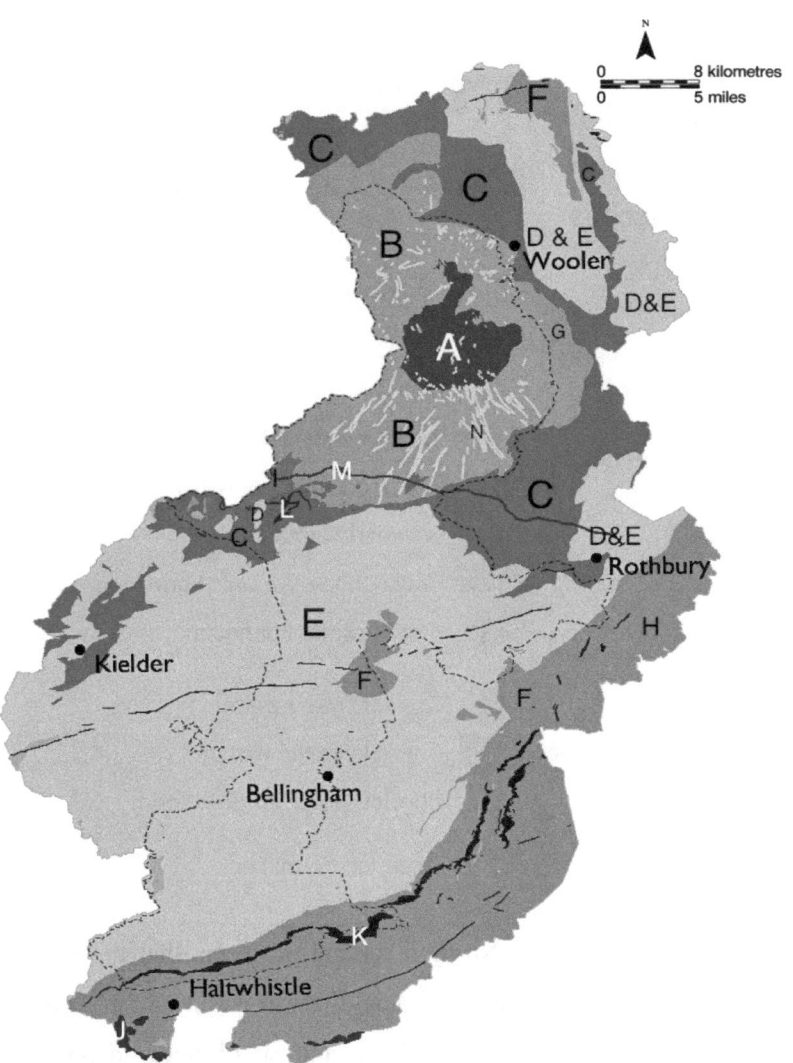

Simplified geological map showing the bedrock in part of Northumberland with a key on the following page. Reproduced in black and white from original coloured map and key in order to show the authors' overlaid letters, all by permission of the British Geological Survey - Permit Number CP/16/003 British Geological Survey © UKRI. All rights reserved.

3

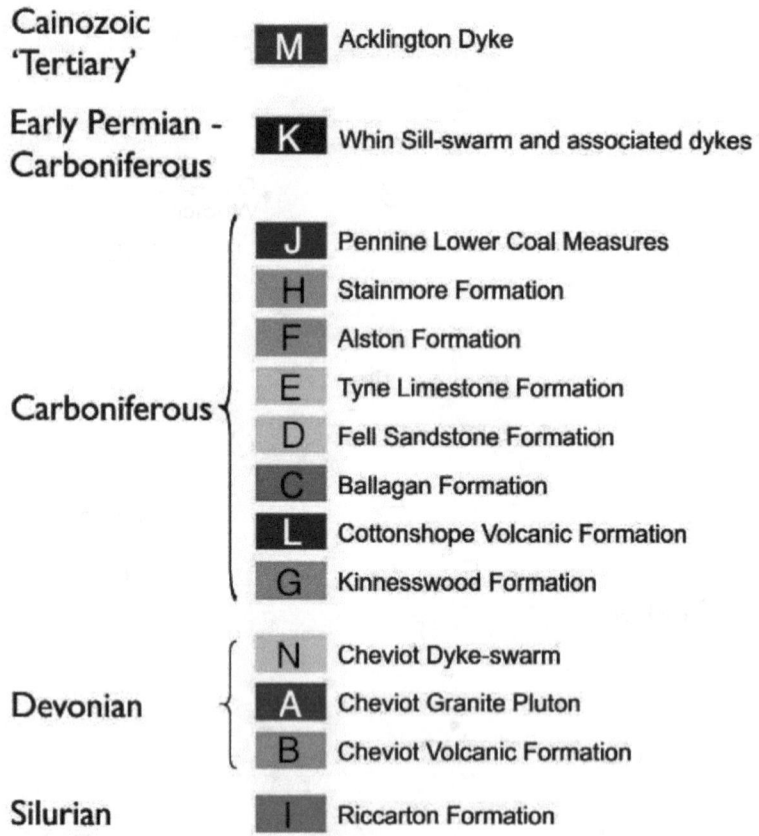

In this area of north Northumberland, it seems that the Cheviot Massif deflected the west to east glacial flow around it on the north and south sides, leaving material in large and small linear deposits as drumlins, megadrumlins and megaflutes. To the east of the Cheviot massif, these Quaternary deposits are glaciofluvial, meaning that the material was left by glacial meltwater. There were also ancient lake deposits such as the soft, red clays across the Milfield Plain, left behind when an ice dam melted during the retreat of the Tweed basin ice-sheet. These clays are hidden by topsoil and muds. Later, substantial alluvial deposits were laid down in our area of study, caused by rivers and their tributaries carving through the glaciofluvial material, mixing it up and spreading it out to form fertile floodplains and terraces. The valley floor of the River Till is a good example of fertile, farming land formed in this way.

In Branxton, Crookham, Etal and Ford, most of the vernacular buildings would have been built of buff-coloured or grey sandstones from the Ballagan Sandstone Formation extracted from local quarries. The thicker-bedded layers of Ballagan sandstone provide excellent building stone but even the thinner-bedded material produces blocks of a size that are suitable for drystone walls or sheepfolds. Sandstone is also known as 'freestone' because it can be easily worked in any direction unlike, for example, slate which splits in one direction. Within the Ballagan sandstone are nodules and beds of dolostones (cementstones). Dolostones or dolomite rocks are thought to derive from limestone (to which they are very similar) by the action of magnesium-rich groundwater. The best example of this to be seen nearby is the whitish- cream rock at Carham, in the form of large boulders on the southern bank of the River Tweed. These were remarked upon when TillVAS was helping with the excavations that took place to the west of Wark Castle in May 2015. *Carham* may derive from the Old English *carr* meaning rocks and *ham* meaning village or homestead.[2]

Some of the buildings in the four villages may have been built from the nearby Fell Sandstone Formation which is characteristically pale grey or buff-coloured and is a good stone if strength is needed for, say, bridge building, where strong ashlar blocks are necessary (see Chapter 3). The small disused quarries to the north and east of Ford probably supplied most of the stone for that village after Lady Waterford was given a life interest in the Estate in 1859 and also after the 1st Baron Joicey purchased the Ford Estate in 1907. Stone from slightly further afield offered a different colour if needed for contrast or other aesthetic reasons. For example, the Fell Sandstone from Doddington Quarry has a pinkish tone that can contrast well with buff or grey and has had wide use in buildings in north Northumberland.

Locally sourced sandstone (buff yellow to grey) in a barn wall near Branxton.

Igneous rock can also be seen in buildings in the villages either as general walling or as individual stones inserted into a sandstone wall. The use as walling is not so common in this area, compared with villages across the Border in Berwickshire. For example, at Gordon, whole buildings are walled in dark, igneous rock. The igneous rocks used might be, firstly, from the intrusive Cheviot Granite Pluton or, secondly, from the extrusive Cheviot Volcanic Formation. The first is a course-grained granite containing reddish-grey and pinkish-grey feldspar (a group of minerals that makes up to 60% of the Earth's crust) with black and yellowish micas with pale grey quartz.

A section of wall constructed wholly of dark igneous rock but, again, the stones vary in colour.

The second volcanic source comprises dark, greenish to blueish, andesite lavas with other elements to it. However, it may be that these types of igneous rocks are to be found more commonly in buildings in the eastern Cheviot Hills rather than in this area. The other type of igneous rock used in building in north Northumberland comes from the Great Whin Sill (marked 'K' on the map on page 3) which comprises dark, grey-black to black, fine to medium-grained, weakly porphyritic (containing one group of crystals much larger than the rest) quartz-dolerites and many other elements. These sill rocks are called 'whinstone'.

Because it is often difficult to distinguish between the different types of igneous rock used in buildings in this area, it is probably more simple to adopt the generic term 'whinstone' for all the dark igneous rocks that we come across and this would seem to comply with local descriptive practice. The example shown on page 7 is a good example of a whole wall constructed of hard whinstone and set in traditional lime mortar.

A section of wall constructed of mixed stone with the occasional piece of whinstone.

The wall shown on page 8 is quite different and, apart from the regular 'quoins' (see chapter 3) on the right of the photo, appears to have been built of colourful, unshaped, random rubble stones that probably came to hand from field gatherings, with the occasional whinstone and with liberal amounts of mortar to fill in the gaps.

For more information on the bedrock geology in and around the villages, please see the Geology Appendix at the end of this book.

2
Building Styles

Branxton, Crookham, Etal, Ford and Heatherslaw are small settlements set in a rural landscape and this is reflected in the character of their buildings. In this and in later chapters we will be looking at houses, farm houses, farm buildings, cottages, barns and other buildings that are all within the parish boundaries or within medieval subdivisions of the parishes known as townships. For example, Branxton is a separate parish whereas Ford parish includes the former townships of Ford, Crookham and Etal. These historic townships are found particularly in the north of England; they may have arisen because it was felt that parishes were too large to administer conveniently but there may have been other reasons to do with land ownerships or divisions. A township would have been administered in the same way as a parish by, for example, appointing officials to oversee the poor and to survey and repair roads and to collect a rate to fund these responsibilities. Townships disappeared during the 19th century and, today, the smallest unit of local government administration is the civil parish.

Over-view: Within the villages, there are buildings that, at one time, were occupied by tradesmen and tradeswomen who were essential to support the rural community, such as blacksmiths, tailors, butchers, milliners, and village shop and post office workers. Many or most of these working buildings have since been converted to residential use, but some of the buildings still show features that give clues to their former use, particularly so where extensions are visible that were once shops attached to cottages.

A former butcher's shop attached to an Edwardian house in Crookham.

Unlike more highly populated urban areas, there were no public or commercial buildings in the four villages that would have had a prestigious character, such as banks, town halls and offices. In a rural area such as this, any 'higher status' buildings with architectural and building design features which reflect their importance, are castles, manor houses, vicarages and churches and these, by their nature, often have period facades and other impressive features. In Branxton can be seen the Grade II listed Church of St. Paul, the Grade II former vicarage and the Grade II listed Branxton House. In Crookham there are the Grade II* listed Pallinsburn House, the Grade II listed The Manse, and the Grade II

18th, 19th & 20th century Grade II* listed Pallinsburn House, Crookham.

14th century Flagpole Tower with later alterations, Grade I listed Ford Castle.

listed Blue Bell Inn. Ford has its magnificent Grade I listed Ford Castle, the Grade II* listed Church of St. Michael and All Angels, the Grade II* listed Lady Waterford Hall, and the Grade II listed Parson's Tower. In Etal there are the Grade I listed Etal Castle, the Grade II* listed Etal Manor, the Grade II listed chapel of St. Mary the Virgin and the Grade II listed former Presbyterian Church. There are other listings for farmhouses, cottages, bridges, gates, walls, fountains, wells, monuments, mileposts and memorials, including the mill, kiln, carthouse and forge at Heatherslaw.

Building styles in the villages vary greatly according to age and architectural trends, by their use, by their status and by the use of local materials. In addition to the listed buildings, there are many buildings that are less grand but which are interesting and noteworthy, such as former schools, school-houses and the many cottages that were built by the landed estates for their outdoor employees or house staff. There were also the reading rooms and other facilities provided for residents in the villages. The varied designs added to the overall look and prestige of the estate, so much so that, for example in Ford and Crookham, 'Waterford' and 'Joicey' plaques can be seen on houses and other buildings to emphasise proprietorial involvement. Over the years, many of the houses built by the estates have been modernised and given extensions. In Crookham and Branxton, houses have been sold off from time to time by the Ford and Etal and Pallinsburn Estates whereas agricultural land in the wider townships has been largely retained. In Ford and Etal, more houses were retained by the estate for leasing to employees and to other tenants.

14th century Grade I listed, Great Tower, Etal Castle.

Grade II listed gates and avenue leading to the Grade II* listed, 18th century Etal Manor that can just be seen in the distance.

Building Styles

Crookham Village Hall completed in 1912 and originally built as a Reading Room.

Plaque on the Lady Waterford Hall, Ford

Joicey plaque on a house in Ford

Some of the estate houses started life as lodges and were designed to enhance the image of the landed estates. Good examples can still be seen, for example, at the two entrances to Pallinsburn House, at Ford and at Etal Manor. The Grade II listed East Lodge (page 17) to Pallinsburn House, built c. 1840, has a swept concave roof, with cast-iron supporting columns and squared stone block construction with ashlar quoins. The present door and windows are not original and it is interesting to compare the two photos on page 17.

Between the First and Second World Wars, municipal housing was introduced into Branxton at Flodden Crescent, first of all in order to house returning ex-servicemen and then, in subsequent years, to provide affordable dwellings for people to rent from the local authority as an alternative to privately owned housing. More recently this stock of former council housing has become owner/occupied under the Government's Right to Buy scheme, introduced in 1980. Since the Second World War, privately-built housing development has occurred in Branxton and Crookham. Modern private housing in Branxton has been in the form of individually designed detached bungalows whereas in Crookham a small estate of bungalows was built at Croft Gardens in a pleasing, generic style that blends in well with the vernacular style of older houses in the village. The situation in Ford and Etal is different because all the land and buildings are still owned by Ford & Etal Estates and none has been sold for speculative development. The neat and tidy buildings and landscaping are maintained by the Estate.

Thus, a wide range of buildings is to be seen in the townships, reflecting a wealth of local history with features which reflect differing building styles and uses. In their own ways, these features are no less interesting than those to be seen on grand buildings in towns and cities—it is just that they are on a different scale. They will still show a 'hierarchy' of building, distinguishing between 'grander' houses and the

Building Styles

East Lodge, Pallinsburn House, today.

East Lodge around the turn of the 19th century, showing the original wrought iron railings and the gates to Pallinsburn House.   **Photo, TillVAS Archives.**

more simple cottages. Within each use category of building this could relate to the status of the owner or occupier but could also be determined by the function of the building, or both.

Examples of this may be seen, say, within a group of farm buildings where the farmhouse will be the dominant building but set apart from barns and other agricultural buildings. The agricultural buildings have their own interest with architectural and building features worth noting as we will see. An example is Crookham Westfield Farmhouse with its superior design details standing well apart from the farm buildings within its own walled garden and yard.

Crookham Westfield Farmhouse.

Building Styles

However as with many farms, this enhanced status for the farmhouse was often only achieved later in the 19th century. According to 19th century Ordnance Survey maps, the farmhouse at Crookham Westfield was built between 1862 and 1898 at the same time as farm cottages were built opposite the farm on the north side of the A697 road. Before that the farmer and the farmworkers would have occupied simple accommodation within the farm buildings, a situation that was common throughout the four villages and outlying hamlets.

At Mardon farm between Crookham and Branxton just south of the Flodden battlefield, is an even grander farmhouse situated in its own grounds with gardens, lawns, orchard and woodland. It is well separated from the utilitarian buildings and has the appearance of a mansion.

Grade II listed Mardon Farmhouse on the Pallinsburn Estate, c. 1840.

18th century & before: Most of the buildings in the villages and in the former townships are built in a vernacular style using local materials and in accordance with local building traditions. The majority were constructed in the 19th century and into the early 20th century but some originated in the 18th century or even earlier either as the 'core' of an enlarged building or in a modified form. Fashions in building design changed a great deal and the earliest buildings that were once thatched were gradually re-roofed in other materials.

There are not very many buildings to be seen that originate before the 18th century apart from the already-mentioned Ford Castle, the Parson's Tower, Etal Castle, the parish churches in Branxton and Ford, Pallinsburn House and Etal Manor (detailed descriptions are outwith the scope of this book). Most 'ordinary' houses and cottages from this and earlier periods would have been flimsily built of timber and cob (mixed clay, straw and small and small stones) or mud with thatched roofs. Some of them would have been of the *longhouse* type divided into two by a through passage, with living room with bedroom off on one side and a byre for the animals on the other side of the passage. The thick, rounded walls of between two and four feet with protective layers of lime plaster or limewash were needed to keep the houses waterproof and to keep in the heat from the open fire. The floors were of beaten mud, bonded perhaps with other agents. On the Solway Plain, there was a bonding agent of bullocks' blood.[3] This may not have been the case in Northumberland and floors here may just have been a mixture of beaten mud and clay. Stone walls began to replace timber and cob from the 17th to the 18th century and brick also became popular, particularly if there were local brickworks and despite a brick tax being imposed in 1784. Thatch was replaced by slates, flags or clay pantiles in the 19th century.

Other examples of 18th century buildings in the villages are worth noting. In Crookham, the former Presbyterian manse dates from around 1750 although it was re-roofed and extended in the 19th century.

The former Presbyterian manse (now The Manse), Crookham, built c. 1750.

The Manse is a substantial stone house set in a large garden and was built to reflect the status of the minister in the community. Some of the external features of the house will be mentioned in the later chapters that deal with building materials and construction techniques.

Opposite The Manse on the other side of the B6353 road are two cottages (originally three), said to be the oldest cottages in Crookham; they may also have been part of a longer terrace.

Old cottages, 2 & 4 Crookham Village, built in the 18th century.

They have been much altered but a hint of the party walls between the original three dwellings can still be seen by looking at the roof slope in the above photo. Close examination of the front wall also reveals where a door to No. 2 has been infilled and part of a window blocked off when the building was altered over the years. These workers' cottages are built in random rubble stonework (see chapter 3) and would originally have been thatched in reed, straw, or perhaps even heather.

Building Styles

18th century cottages in Crookham roofed in pantiles and thatch, c.1900.
Photo, TillVAS Archives

The left-hand cottages in the photo on page 22 may be the same cottages pictured in the photo (circa 1900) above. The right-hand cottage above is roofed in thatch and bears some similarity to the cottage shown on the right on page 22 although there is no chimney-stack on the roof of that cottage. The cottage on page 24 is said to have been a blacksmith's cottage with the distinctive workshop window to the left of the simple front door suggesting that the blacksmith's shop was behind it with what was probably a living area and a bedroom to the right. A grinding stone

23

and a wooden workshop give additional likelihood to this supposition. The thatch looks traditionally rustic with an irregular line at the eaves.

A possible 18th century blacksmith's cottage, Crookham, c. 1900.
Photo, TillVAS archives

Another example of an 18th century building but one which is quite different in style is what is known as the 'Apple Store' in the grounds of Pallinsburn House. This Grade II listed building has handmade brickwork and thin window frames suggesting a date in the early 18th century but with a 19th century door and porch. The building is quite unusual in that a pedimented gable was added in the late 18th century with a blank 'Venetian window'. The pediment can be seen standing well above the roof slope on the right of the photo. The nearby joiner's workshop has an identical blank Venetian window and pediment except that a 10-pane workshop window has been inserted at a later date (see page 68).

The 18th century Apple Store in the grounds of Pallinsburn House.

Perhaps the oldest surviving building in Crookham, the earliest part of which probably dates from the first half of the 18th century, is the Grade II listed Crookham Cottage, now known as the Coach House. This is situated south of the entrance to Crookham Village on the A697 road and was formerly three cottages. The left-hand section has a steeply sloping roof that suggests that it was originally thatched. The English Heritage listing in 1988 states that the right-hand section of the building may date to circa 1830 and the staircase in the older section to circa 1810.

Crookham Cottage (The Coach House) photo copyright © Peter Ryder

Another building illustrating yet another style and surviving from the late 18th century is the Grade II listed Blue Bell Inn at Crookham. This is a former coaching inn which is built largely of brick with later sandstone extensions and having a modern restaurant extension at the rear. The main gables have 'tumbled in' brickwork which produces an attractive patterned effect. Across England, brick became more widespread from the 18th century onward, its use helped by better road, canal and, later, rail transport. In this area, there was an abundance of natural stone and brick, the latter often being used on cost grounds due to the presence of nearby brick and tileworks. Brick would also have been used for aesthetic reasons and there were practical reasons for its use as we discuss later in relation to chimney stacks.

Grade II listed Blue Bell Inn, Crookham.

In Ford and Etal villages there are few buildings surviving from the 18th century and before, apart from Ford and Etal Castles, the Parson's Tower adjacent to Ford Church, Ford Parish Church itself and Etal Manor. However at Etal, it is worth mentioning the Grade II listed former Presbyterian church and manse near Etal Castle. Strictly speaking, the church dates from 1800 but it was rebuilt at that time with lower courses of larger stone which suggest that these survive from an earlier 18th century building. Apart from this, most of the walls are built of random rubble with ashlar quoins although the upper part of the gable shows more regular stonework built roughly to courses. The former church now houses English Heritage's exhibition about the Battle of Flodden as well as local historical information.

Grade II listed former Presbyterian Church and manse at Etal.

The former Presbyterian manse (now a house) is dated to the mid 18th century and can just be seen to the right of the church in the photo above. The walls are built of large, squared blocks of dressed stone and these give the impression that they might have been re-used from Etal Castle.

Building Styles

Also to be seen in Etal is a building near the river possibly one of the former mill buildings (the mill itself is no longer there). It is tempting to think that this building may originate in the 18th century as Etall (sic) Mills appears on a Land Tax schedule for 1806.[4] The building has recently been used as a joinery showroom and store.

Probably one of the former mill buildings at Etal, 18th?/19th century.

Ford parish includes the hamlet of Heatherslaw which comprises cottages, a working corn-mill and mill-shop with a cafe, visitors' centre, and gift-shop in the former mill buildings. These are all on the west bank of the River Till whilst, on the east bank of the river, are buildings now associated with the Heatherslaw Light Railway. Ford & Etal Estates record that the Grade II-listed mill was rebuilt as a 'double mill' in 1768 on the site of a watermill said to have existed before 1300 and owned by the Ford Estate since 1376. The mill buildings were enlarged in around 1830. The present railway buildings were used originally by the Ford Forge which made spades and farming tools. It is said that, by the early 1800s, seven water wheels were in action with thirty houses along the river banks.[5]

Confirmation that the forge was in existence by 1776 is provided by W. Hutchinson who states

> The situation of the Forge is romantic, and the whole scene picturesque. The water to supply the wheels is collected by a dam, and forms a fine canal, from whence it breaks over the wear in a beautiful cascade; and being intercepted in its lower course by rocks and hillocks, divides itself into several streams. The buildings for the forge, as you look up the river, lay to the left; on the opposite side is a water-corn-mill: the vale seen above the canal consists of cultivated and enclosed grounds, which are highly contrasted by the lofty eminences which bound the prospect, finely broken and irregular, through which the light streams, and gives a singular beauty to the offscape: these at the extreme point of view are overlooked by Cheviot, awfully supreme and majestic, on whose brow heavy vapours are generally seen suspended.[6]

Today the light railway buildings and Heatherslaw Mill are picturesque reminders of 18th and 19th century rural industry.

Building Styles

Above and below: Grade II-listed Heatherslaw Mill.

Grade II-listed former cart shed and former corn-drying kiln with stores across the lane from Heatherslaw Mill. 18th century and later.

Grade II-listed buildings at the former Ford Forge. 18th century and later.

Building Styles

The photo at the top of page 32 provides evidence of how buildings (in this case, working buildings) change over time. The doors of the former cart shed on the left have been infilled with modern windows, square pillars and wooden lintels. The building on the right which forms part of the former corn-drying kiln and storage may have had an additional storey added at some time. There has certainly been considerable alteration, with the lower section of the gable being built largely of random rubble whinstone. Above this is another section of random rubble sandstone with a later window and above this a section comprising horizontal brickwork with 'tumbled-in' brickwork below the sloping gable parapets. A triangular, timber dovecote screen has been set into the horizontal brickwork.

19th century: Most of the buildings we see today in the four villages and townships were built in the 19th century and we are fortunate in that the late Georgian and Victorian eras provide us with such a wide variety of interesting buildings and building styles.

The period from the end of the 18th century until the middle of the 19th century was one of substantial demographic change in England. The population increased from around 6 million in 1750 to over 16 million by 1851. This had to be supported by an increase in agricultural production and this was stimulated by a number of factors such as higher grain prices from 1750 onwards, peaking during the Napoleonic Wars which ended in 1815, along with improved transport facilities such as canals and better roads. There were increases in land values and there was additional involvement by government which set up a Board of

Agriculture in 1793 to commission county studies into best practice. The Parliamentary Enclosure Acts were at their peak between 1800 and 1815 (although in Northumberland, enclosure was mostly by private agreement between landowners) and many small farmers suffered hardship by losing their rights over common land. The expenses of enclosure associated with fencing, hedging and ditching and sometimes the construction of new steadings, increased the incentive to small owners and tenants to sell to larger landowners or to give up their leases, especially if rents were increased at the same time.[7]

In Northumberland, the landscape was generally dominated by large estates which, in the 19th century, were often enriched by both 'old money' and 'new money' owners transferring profits from the coal industry (particularly in this area) but also from other types of industry, into their estates. The Industrial Revolution from the end of the 18th century onwards caused a large movement of population from the countryside into the towns. However it is interesting to note that although the proportion of agricultural workers declined from a little over one in three of the population in 1815 to about one in six by the middle of the century, the total number of farm labourers increased by about one million by 1850.[8]

The new landscape of rectangular fields and larger-scale farming, combined with new farming methods, did bring about an increase in crop yields. This was helped by improvements in livestock, improvement of soils due to liming and marling, the introduction of improved grasses and winter feed-crops, better seed production, better

Building Styles

farm machinery, more efficient distribution of manure from over-wintered livestock and the introduction of clay-pipe drainage. In this part of north Northumberland, the new farming practices introduced by the Culley brothers in the first part of the 19th century did much to help livestock and arable production. The condition of agriculture generally, improved gradually from the 1830s onwards and even more so after the repeal of the Corn Laws in 1846. After about 1860, farming entered a depression but the wealth created in the urban economy through free trade enabled Britain to become the largest importer of agricultural produce in the world by the 1930s.[9]

It was the changes mentioned above that determined the character of buildings in the townships during the 19th century. Most of the farm buildings were built or altered and farmhouses and farm workers' cottages were built as we mentioned above on pages 18 and 19. There were also great changes to buildings in the villages as many of these buildings were linked to their agricultural surroundings.

The Old Vicarage at Branxton was built from specifications drawn up in 1837, the first year of Queen Victoria's reign but it still retains features reminiscent of the Georgian period, such as the window and roof designs. Although quite grand, regard was given to the cost to be borne by the church so instead of building in exposed and more expensive coursed stonework, the random rubble walling was rendered and painted. This does create a pleasing appearance. The porch is not original and it detracts from the arched, stonework door surround.

Old Vicarage, Branxton, 1837.

The majority of cottages in the villages would originally have been single-storey buildings, such as the cottages at Crookham shown in the photo on page 22. During the 19th century, improving standards led to the building of one and a half-storey cottages such as those at the 'Blue Row' at Branxton. More expensive two-storey houses were built for the middle-class occupiers of Branxton Villa and the (School) Master's House at Crookham, both shown on page 38. Larger houses such as the Old Vicarage shown above and the substantial farmhouses mentioned earlier, are in keeping with the status of their owners (or tenant farmers) in the community. Ford Castle, Etal Manor and Pallinsburn House reflected the status of their aristocratic or gentry landowners.

Building Styles

The Blue Row, Branxton, today. Compare this with the photo below.

The Blue Row, Branxton, c. 1900   Photo, TillVAS archives

Aspects of Buildings & Monuments: Branxton, Crookham, Etal, Ford

The two-storey Branxton Villa, built 1847.

The two-storey Master's House, Crookham, built in squared, coursed ashlar.

Building Styles

The houses, cottages and other buildings in Ford have a quite different character from those in Branxton, Crookham and Etal. Most of the 19th houses in Ford are built of a grey sandstone whereas the early 20th century houses are of a warmer-coloured sandstone. However, some grey sandstone is to be found in Branxton and Crookham; for example, the former school and adjoining schoolhouse in Crookham are built entirely of grey sandstone and, in other buildings, the quoins and door and window surrounds in grey sandstone contrast with the predominating buff colour.

Many of the buildings in Ford were built in the 1860s during the lifetime of Louisa, Marchioness of Waterford (1818-1891) after her permanent move to Ford Castle following the death of her husband, Henry, 3rd Marquess of Waterford in 1854. Lady Waterford created what amounted to a 'model village'; at the same time she carried out many philanthropic works in the neighbourhood and painted the Pre-Raphaelite-style murals around the walls of what was then Ford School and is now the Lady Waterford Hall. The people depicted in the murals were living in the village or living and working at the nearby Ford Moss colliery. There were some very ornate and interesting building styles and features created during Lady Waterford's time and three examples can be seen on pages 40 and 41 which further illustrate her artistry.

Later buildings in Ford were commissioned by the 1st Baron Joicey (1846-1936) who continued to manage and conserve the village during the remainder of the 19th century and the first part of the 20th century.

Aspects of Buildings & Monuments: Branxton, Crookham, Etal, Ford

Lady Waterford Hall, Ford Village.

Grade II listed Jubilee Cottage, Ford, built 1887.

Grade II listed former blacksmith's forge at Ford Village, built 1863.

Jubilee Cottage has a Royal Doulton terracotta plaque above the front door with Queen Victoria's head in profile commemorating the Queen's diamond jubilee in 1887. The door surround of the former Blacksmith's forge at Ford is a distinctive and whimsical feature built during Lady Waterford's time. The forge was in use until the 1970s.

The earliest 19th century houses or cottages to survive in Etal are two semi-detached houses fronting the road that runs down from the castle to the river. They are close to the site of the old Etal corn mill and may have been occupied by mill workers. However, a local legend suggests that the buildings may have originally been a public house that was strategically placed just above the ford that crosses the River Till to New Etal and beyond.

Early 19th century houses at Etal. The workshop and store on page 29 can be seen at the right of the photo.

Just above these houses, also next to the road running down to the ford at Etal, is the former Parsonage (built sometime between 1862 and 1881) which, in the late 19th century, was occupied by the incumbent of the Chapel of St. Mary the Virgin. The chapel, situated off the drive to Etal Manor, was founded and endowed by Lady Augusta FitzClarence, in memory of her husband Lord Frederick FitzClarence who died in 1853 whilst Commander-in-Chief of the Army in India, The chapel is built of attractive pink and buff banded sandstone with a roof of Westmoreland slates. It was designed by William Butterfield and built in 1856-1858 and houses the remains of Lord and Lady FitzClarence and also their daughter and Lord Frederick's aide-de-camp.

Building Styles

Chapel of the Blessed Virgin Mary, Etal, built 1856/58.

Former Parsonage, Etal, built after 1862.

From the 1920s there ceased to be a separate incumbent of St. Mary's Chapel, Etal and the Rector of Ford also became Chaplain of St. Mary's in a combined parish renamed Ford and Etal.[10]

20th and 21st centuries: In the Edwardian period, before the First World War, there was a change in architectural styles with Gothic or Tudor features appearing, such as vernacular, solid forms, large chimneys, large stone window cills, stone mullions, exposed decorative timber, deep porches and steep roofs. This was embodied in buildings influenced by the Arts and Crafts movement originally developed in the 1860s and inspired by the designer, William Morris (1834-1896). It was continued by other architects and designers into the 20th century. The Arts and Crafts style encompassed the ideas of simple forms, natural motifs, the use of natural materials and the vernacular forms of the British countryside. This style also appeared in interior design and furniture. Its influence can be seen in a number of properties, particularly in Ford and Crookham and an example can be seen on page 45.

It was mentioned above that after the First World War, municipal housing was built in Branxton and, more recently, private development occurred in Branxton and Crookham. Ford did not expand in the same way and Ford Estate maintained the character of the existing houses in Ford Village as well as that of the farms on the estate but made improvements over the years to reflect rising standards of living. This policy continues today with Ford & Etal Estates initiating and carrying out innovative projects to adapt, refurbish, enlarge and improve access to property in Ford and Etal for existing or potential tenants.

An Edwardian house in Ford Village showing the influence of the Arts and Crafts movement.

In Etal village an enlightened policy of improvement was initiated by the 1st Baron Joicey during the first part of the 20th century. At that time the cottages in the village (with some exceptions such as the post office and the rectory) were single-storey, whitewashed stone buildings with thatched roofs. The accommodation was primitive with each cottage consisting of one or two rooms of simple layout and design and with privies located behind the cottages. Lord Joicey decided that the buildings on both sides of the street should be demolished and replaced by one and a half or two-storey houses. There are plaques on the front of the houses recording construction dates of 1935, 1936 and 1937 (the last during the lifetime of the 2nd Baron Joicey). In the 1950s other plaques were installed on houses in Etal when rebuilding was resumed after the Second World War by the 3rd Baron Joicey. The traditional white-painted walls were maintained for many of the houses and thatched roofs were installed on two of the cottages and on the Black Bull public house.

The entrance to Etal Village today, showing some of the white-painted houses and the thatched Black Bull public house.

Buildings in the 20th and 21st centuries have often been built in a vernacular style and a simple example of this is the former Power House at Etal shown on page 47. It was built in the 1920s close to a former mill building shown on page 29 and, at first glance, gives the appearance of being of contemporary construction. The electricity was used to power equipment in Etal Manor and also at New Etal across the River Till and, later, lighting and simple equipment in Etal village.[11] Water flowed from the River Till and a generator fed power to batteries in the former mill building which became known as the Battery House. When there was insufficient water, a diesel engine in the Power House was linked to a separate generator which fed power to the Battery House.

Former Power House at Etal, 20th century, to the right of one of the former mill buildings known later as the Battery House.

In chapter 6, we will be touching on factors to consider when trying to date buildings. Buildings are not always what they appear to be at first glance.

3

Wall Construction

This chapter looks at, firstly, the stonework used for building construction in the villages and then looks at brickwork. In the stone quarries (most of which would have been local) or in the workshops, the stonemasons cut and worked the stone into two kinds of building block, firstly, dressed sandstone in regular rectangular blocks and, secondly, roughly squared sandstone blocks to be used for less formal walling. In addition, builders used stones gathered from the fields, uncut or perhaps lightly trimmed, for use in random rubble walling. An important rule is that, because sandstone is a sedimentary stone, i.e. laid down millions of years ago in a series of deposited bedding layers at the bottom of a sea, lake or river, the building stones should always be built into a wall with the bedding layers or planes at right angles to the face of the wall, to resist weathering. This usually means as horizontal bedding planes, but they can be vertical for some features. These bedding planes can be seen in the photograph of a worn section of wall (page 49). If such stones were laid with the planes parallel to the wall face, the planes could easily split away like cards falling from a playing card pack.

Dressed sandstone of regular sized blocks was either polished to create a smooth surface known as ashlar or tooled to give an attractive decorated surface. Dressed stonework is stone that has been worked to a desired shape, with ashlar having the very finest mortar joints. A very early example of ashlar walling at Birdoswald is shown on page 49.

Wall Construction

Worn, sandstone wall showing horizontal bedding planes.

Ashlar walling at Birdoswald Roman Fort, Hadrian's Wall.

Ashlar walling can often be found on classical public buildings; we do not have these in the four villages and even the large mansions, manses, parsonages or vicarages tend to have regular dressed stonework rather than ashlar, or they have rendered walls covering the stone or, in the case of Pallinsburn, built of good quality brickwork. The image of Birdoswald masonry, even though it is outside our area, is included simply because it is such fine work with closely interlocking stones and fine joints.

A section of wall at The Manse, Crookham.

The Manse, Crookham can provide examples of regular sized dressed and tooled stonework on the south elevation and on the impressive garden walls but over the course of time, there has been weathering and patching up of mortar joints. The mortar joints (see page 50) are wider than they would be for a building with ashlar masonry but this was never intended to be anything other than a good, solidly built country house befitting the status of the parson. Apart from some piecemeal patching up in cement, the joints retain the softer look of lime mortar and this, together with the warm-colour of the weathered blocks, gives a feeling of age and history to the stonework which also provides an excellent backdrop for climbing plants.

The following photograph shows a section of wall on Crookham Village Hall that comes nearest to the finely dressed ashlar stonework that might be seen on a building of high quality and status. The building blocks are finely dressed and the mortar joints are thin, so it is necessary to use a coloured mortar that shows the narrowness of the joints, yet defines the ashlar stonework. The blocks are perfectly 'squared off', with a smooth finish and are of identical height in regular courses.

It is sometimes possible to find what amounts to a kind of 'deceit' where wide joints between blocks are filled with mortar of the same colour as the stonework, but with a narrow channel incised into the joints and filled with a hard fillet of, say, putty, lime or chalk of a contrasting colour (usually white or grey). The technique gives a false impression of narrow pointing between ashlar blocks. This form of pointing is known as 'tuck pointing'. So far this has not been discovered in Branxton and Crookham but there are examples of other forms of pointing (to be described later on) which would not find favour with traditionalists, but which are obviously enjoyed by the owners of the properties.

Here is another example of dressed stonework (but not ashlar, except for the quoins) on the United Reformed Church, Crookham.

Section of wall on Crookham United Reformed Church, built 1932-1933.

It is rather unusual because of the angled quoins which relate to the 1930s Art Deco architectural style of the building. Also, the dressed stonework is not set in regular courses and the blocks are offset and of different sizes and colours. They are all regular however, if not always rectangular. The stonework is making a statement and although it reflects the high status of the building, it also honours the individual 1930s style created by the architect.

Other buildings in the two villages and the surrounding countryside show the many gradations between prestigious ashlar laid in regular courses, and cottage walls of un-coursed masonry in what is termed 'random rubble'. Random rubble might simply be field gatherings that have received little or no tooling, but the stones might still be laid in courses, 'random rubble built to courses' as opposed to stonework not laid to courses.

The difference may be illustrated by the following photographs. The first, on page 54, shows stones of different sizes, some perhaps more 'random' than others, because the wall also includes some re-used stones. However, they are laid roughly in courses with continuous horizontal beds. In random rubble built to courses, the strength of the wall is created by the wall layer's skill (which would be crucial if it were dry-stone walling) and, as in this case, also by the binding medium provided by the mortar. If we compare this with the Roman masonry shown on page 49, the strength of the Roman wall depends entirely on the regular shape of the stones and the precision with which they are laid rather than relying entirely on a binding medium.

Random rubble walling with the rubble built roughly to courses.

In the second example, seen in a boundary wall in Branxton on page 55, the stones are still random and even in irregular courses but the strength of the wall depends to a greater extent on the mortar which is more visible on the face as a means of infilling gaps in the stone. In this case, the wall had an opening at one time that has been infilled with other unshaped stones. The simple stone surround suggests that this might have provided ventilation perhaps to a building behind, which is now provided by the small, gridded opening, or perhaps it was a hatch or an opening for a chute of some kind. One of the fascinations about looking at old buildings, is trying to work out the way in which they were used and the purpose of features that can be seen in their construction.

A random rubble wall in Branxton with an infilled opening.

All the stonework on the older houses in the villages would have been laid in lime mortar, easily recognised by its soft and gritty, often flecked, appearance. In recent years, repairs and repointing have most often been carried out using cement mortar, which is cheaper but gives a harder and smoother finish. Unfortunately, as well as looking not quite right on old buildings, the use of cement mortar can be a false economy as its strength does not accommodate small movements of the building without cracking. Also its impermeability prevents the escape of moisture which has seeped into the stonework (particularly so with brickwork) and cannot then find its way out through the joints; this can lead to internal dampness and stone or brick decay including very visible surface 'spalling'. The use of more expensive 'breathable' lime mortar will often be the cheapest option in the long run and it will always give a more attractive finish. An example showing dressed stone with appropriately under-stated lime mortar can be seen in the image below.

Dressed stone built to courses with ashlar quoins and lime mortar.

A preference for the use of lime mortar over cement mortar is not everyone's view and the question of practicality, cost and individual taste will always be a valid consideration. In the image on page 57, an uncoursed, random rubble wall in Branxton was probably originally laid in lime mortar but has since been pointed with cement mortar in a technique known as 'ribbon pointing' where the mortar stands proud of the stone. If the wall had been built to courses, the horizontal and vertical pointing would be known as 'strap pointing'. Aesthetically, it should be the stonework that dominates, not the mortar. This is a subjective view, however.

Ribbon pointing of random rubble walling, Branxton.

Shaped stones may be dressed or surfaced with a variety of tooled finishes on their faces, the simplest probably being 'droving' or 'broaching' which consists of a series of fairly narrow, horizontal, almost parallel cut lines produced by a hammer and a broad-faced, toothed chisel or mason's 'boaster'. Another common finish is 'stugging' where the face of the stone is covered by depressions made by a mason's 'punch', which is a special type of hammer. In the photo below, there are examples of both types of finish, in this example from Crookham. The dressed stones laid in courses have all been tooled with narrow parallel droving lines whereas the two blocks in the middle of the picture have been roughly stugged, the combination of both producing a contrasting, decorative effect.

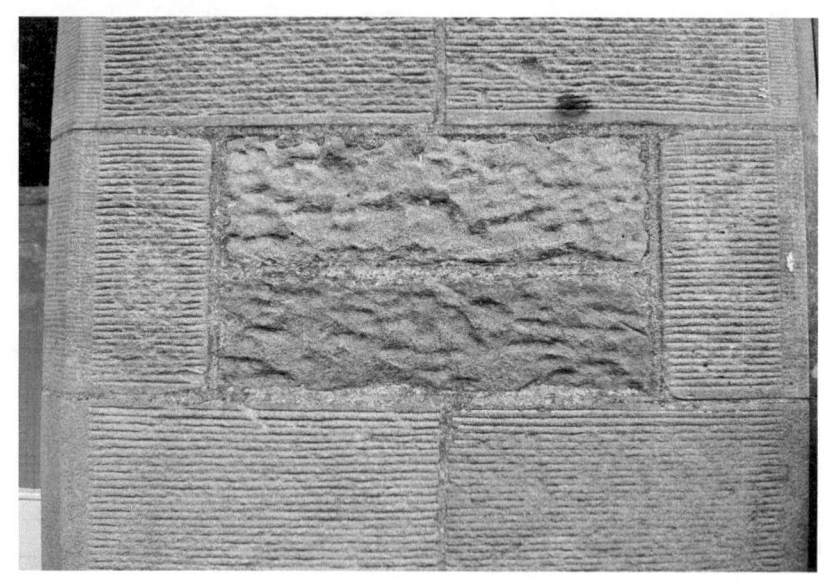

Droving (or broaching) with inset stugged stones.

The following photo shows a mixed wall of squared, stugged stones with some random rubble. The height and width of stones within the courses is irregular and the level of the courses has been made up using smaller stones to infill the horizontal gaps between courses and the vertical gaps between stones. The smaller stones used to make up the height of a course are known as 'pinnings' and those used for infilling vertical spaces between stones are called 'snecks'. In the photo, some three or four snecks can be seen bedded in thick cement mortar in the top left-hand corner and two pinnings can be seen in the middle right, again heavily pointed in cement mortar.

Snecks, pinnings and stugging.

Snecks and pinnings may be used for decorative as well as practical reasons but, in this case, any decorative effect is negated by the cement mortar. There are many other more elaborate toolings to the surface of building stones and also to the joints between them, such as 'rustication' created by wide, recessed joints in masonry, but these appear in town and city locations and there are few examples in the four villages.

There are rusticated quoins at Etal Manor and the photo below shows an example of rustication at Ford; it is a technique often seen on the walls of banks or other prominent public buildings. This is an 18th century example showing the sunken joints cut at an angle of 45 degrees in order to produce a 'V' joint. Rustication is associated with the classical style of architecture and gives an impression of prestige and strength.

Rustication on a gate pier at St. Michael's and All Angels Church, Ford.

The next photo shows a good example of 'vermiculation' to be seen on alternate quoins to the side of the gateway at Ford Castle. It is so called because, in Latin, 'vermiculus' means 'little worm' and it is thought that the decoration often resembles worms, worm casts or worm tracks. In this case, the resemblance is not quite so apparent.

An 18th century ashlar wall at Ford Castle with a false gun port and vermiculation on the quoins of the gateway built during the Delaval period.

Random rubble walling, as well as ashlar and dressed stonework, is often enhanced by incorporating ashlar or other dressed stones known as 'quoins' at the corners of buildings. As well as providing decorative enhancement, there is also an important practical reason for this because it is necessary to provide strong and sharp corners to a building to provide strength and stability. The long and short faces of the quoins often alternate for decorative effect. The quoins in the photo below are of light sandstone which contrast well with the dark whinstone of the wall of the Well House in Branxton. The quoins have a stugged tooling and alternate between long faces and short faces (in Scotland, known as outbands and inbands).

Pale sandstone quoins at the corner of a whinstone wall at Branxton).

Squared blocks or 'rybats' are also placed around door or window openings in order to give straight-edged surrounds to those openings for easier joinery installation and for the sake of appearance. Again, like quoins, the rybats often alternate, long face/short face, or they may be formed as uniform raised surrounds or have some more elaborate finish. Stones used for quoins, window and door surrounds often have tooled 'margins'. The example already used on page 59 and reproduced again here, shows, unusually, margins down the left and right edges of the rybats. The horizontal droving on the narrow margins on the left-hand edges provides a continuous definition at the corner of, in this case, a window. A similar effect would apply to margins on quoins. Margins may be droved or they may be left plain. The use of margins has a decorative effect and here, the droving provides a contrast to the stugging.

Droved margins on the edges of stugged window rybats.

So far, we have only discussed the use of stone for building in north Northumberland because, historically, it was the main building material in this area and builders were able to take advantage of the plentiful supply of local stone. There was also local limestone for making lime mortar, as evidenced by the large number of lime kilns in the area to the north and west of Lowick, and the well-known ones at Lindisfarne Castle.

In other parts of England, brickwork was in evidence from Tudor times. Examples can be seen in grand palaces and mansions such as Hampton Court Palace and East Barsham Manor in Norfolk which exhibit intricate, moulded, shaped, and patterned brickwork in elaborate designs including the characteristic, 'twisted' chimney stacks. From the 17th century onwards, bricks were used more generally in the construction of houses in certain parts of England. In fact, Flemish merchants had settled in East Anglia as early as the 13th century and introduced their brickmaking techniques to the area. Brickwork became more popular for general building in the 18th and 19th centuries despite the imposition of brick taxes between 1784 and 1850. This popularity was helped by the invention of the pugmill which mixed the clays to an even consistency.

In north Northumberland there was also an increasing use of brickwork during the 18th and 19th centuries. Supply in this area was helped by the existence of local brickworks such as the former Flodden Brick and Tileworks established in 1768 and the plentiful supplies of local coal for firing.[12] Also, during the 19th century the rapid growth of railways provided quicker and better distribution with, consequently, cheaper costs. Brick was used for outhouses, chimney stacks and garden walls and there are good examples of the latter use to be seen in the large, walled garden at Etal and in the garden walls at Pallinsburn and The Manse, Crookham. Brickwork was also used for major projects such as Pallinsburn House (including outbuildings such as the Apple Store shown on page 25) and for the 18th century Blue Bell coaching inn (page 27).

18th century brickwork at Pallinsburn House, Crookham. Each section of the pre-metric rule is 6ins.

The hand-made bricks at Pallinsburn are dark-red (with many variations) with firing cracks and irregular sizes and surfaces but with a very pleasing appearance. In the past, hand-made bricks were produced in different sizes in different regions whereas modern machine-made bricks in Britain are made to a standard metric size of 215mm × 102.5mm

× 65mm. The brick taxes mentioned on page 64 had an effect because in 1784, bricks were taxed by number, causing brickmakers and builders to increase their size in order to reduce tax liability. After 1803 the tax was by volume which caused smaller bricks to be made thus producing more bricks for a given amount of the clay and sand mix. In the 18th century, Parliament specified a brick size of 8½ins × 4ins × 2½ins and, from around 1840, manufacturers widely adopted a size of 9ins × 4½ins × 2½ins. This remained the standard size until replaced in 1970 by the metric size stated above.

A gable wall with a variation of English Garden Wall Bond (see next page), Church House, Crookham.

The most common brick bonds to be seen in England are English Bond (alternate rows of stretchers and headers) which was popular until the late 17th century, Flemish Bond (alternate headers and stretchers in each row) which was most popular after the late 17th century and English Garden Wall Bond (three rows of stretchers to one row of headers) which was particularly common in the north of England from the late 18th century onwards with many examples in this area. In the photo on page 66, the 1908 gable wall of the former Presbyterian Church Officer's House, Crookham has a variation of English Garden Wall Bond with four rows of stretchers to one row of headers. The modern wall in the foreground is built in the conventional English Garden Wall Bond.

There are many other brick bonds and variations of bonds and brickwork was also used in a decorative way using bricks of different colours to form lozenges, chevrons, herring-bone patterns and projecting courses, an effect known as 'diapering'. Dark blue engineering bricks can produce useful contrasts for patterning when combined with other colours. There are not many local examples of decorative brickwork although there are examples of brickwork being combined with stonework window, door and other surrounds to create a pleasing result.

The top photo on page 68 shows the rear gable wall of the 18th century Joiner's Workshop at Pallinsburn showing brickwork in Flemish Bond, a bull's eye opening and a false Venetian window (see pages 24/25). The 10-paned window is not original. The bottom photo shows 'tumbled-in' brickwork at the Blue Bell Inn, Crookham. This is not only decorative but provides straight edges for laying and supporting the stone gable parapets. The gable parapets give increased strength at the top of the gable and weather protection for the brick edges below.

The Joiner's Workshop at Pallinsburn combining stone and brick for architectural effect. Note the blank 'Venetian window' with later inset window.

'Tumbled in' brickwork at the Blue Bell Inn, Crookham.

Wall Construction

Because of the regularity of brick courses, strength is provided at the corners by interlocking bricks and overlapping brick courses without the need for stone quoins. The absence of quoins can be seen in the photographs on page 68. However, stone quoins (and rybats, lintels and cills) were incorporated when necessary in order to provide a decorative contrast between brick and stone, for example at Jubilee Cottages on the Pallinsburn estate.

Jubilee Cottages, Pallinsburn Estate, showing brickwork contrasting with the stonework at quoins, lintels, rybats and cills.

The use of timber or earth (cob) as external wall building materials is not discussed in this context because they do not often survive into the 21st century in north Northumberland compared, say, with the south and west of England. Even before the rebuilding of thatched 'hovels'* in the four villages and their hinterlands by the landed estates in the 19th and 20th centuries, stone had largely replaced any timber, wattle and daub, or cob for building external walls in this area because stone was so readily available. Even with older farm buildings (which generally only survive from the 18th and 19th centuries in our area) the external walls are invariably of stone.

*In north Northumberland, 'hovel' was a description meaning a small, humble, thatched, terraced cottage without facilities. It was not necessarily a dirty or squalid place, just a labourer's very basic dwelling.

4
Doors and Windows

Just as the harmony of a human face is determined by its features, so that of an old building is dependent upon the style and positioning of its doors and windows. Alter one or the other and the unique aspect will be destroyed, as happens so often when period doors and windows are replaced by modern 'equivalents' during the course of repair or alteration.

Mardon Farmhouse, Crookham c. 1847.

Taking a close look at the frontage of the mid 19th century farmhouse at Mardon with its scored stucco and stone-dressed frontage, we see that the house is given life by the symmetrical large, twelve-sash windows on either side of the period front door. If the windows or the door were to be replaced by undivided windows or by modern units in non-traditional materials, the effect would be to give the building's 'face' a blank 'stare' or even worse. Another example is the former vicarage at Branxton but, in this case, it might be helpful to disregard the portico which was added later and to just see the five windows and the traditional door and overlight set in the arched stone surround. Both Mardon farmhouse and the former Branxton vicarage present distinctive characters through the symmetry and styles of their architectural 'faces'.

The Old Vicarage, Branxton, 1837.

Doors and Windows

Doors: Although none of the buildings in the villages is within a Conservation Area which would give them additional planning protection, we have seen that many have been placed on the Statutory List of Buildings of Special Architectural or Historic Interest. This means that they cannot be demolished, extended or altered without listed building consent from the local planning authority. The protection extends to features such as external doors and windows which cannot be replaced by unacceptable modern materials such as uPVC or aluminium. Even if an old building is not listed, it would be quite inappropriate to alter the appearance and character of a building in this way. Unfortunately, we see many examples of such inadvertent 'vandalism'.

With or without protection, there are some interesting doors and windows to be seen in the villages. The photograph on the left shows a 19th century four-panelled door in the front elevation of The Manse at Crookham. The door construction comprises the four panels (the upper panels longer than the lower panels) with two vertical 'stiles' (or 'styles') forming the frames of the door. There are three horizontal 'rails', the top, middle and bottom rails that connect with the stiles and there are vertical 'muntins' that connect the top rail to the middle rail and the middle rail to the bottom rail. There is a simple, over-door light whereas, in the illustration below, there is an elegant fanlight above the door. This is the door of the former school at Crookham; the door and fanlight have since been replaced but the new fanlight retains the same pattern. True fanlights originated in the 18th century from about 1720 onwards and the most elaborate lights, with thin glazing-bars or tracery are associated particularly with Georgian architecture, although there are many Victorian designs after 1837. The earliest glazing bars were of wood, but lead or wrought iron was used later on in order to create delicate or curved patterns.

There are not very many examples of what might be described as imposing doors in the villages and the surrounding countryside but one would be the early 20th century door and surround built in Jacobean style during Major Charles Mitchell's substantial alterations at Pallinsburn House.[13] By contrast, the porch at St. Paul's Church, Branxton, built in 1935, has denticulated and chevroned arches and columns, in Romanesque style; this was an 1849 feature reset from the nave's south wall and said to be a copy of the 12th century original.[14]

Doors and Windows

Door in sandstone surround with stone and leaded-pane overlight on the north elevation of Pallinsburn House, Crookham.

Porch door with triple chevron and dentilated arches and supporting columns at St. Paul's Church, Branxton.

There are two doors on the front elevation of the Lady Waterford Hall at Ford which in themselves could not be described as imposing because they are quite simple paled doors. However, they are set into rather monumental porches of ashlar sandstone with dentilated corbels and raised quoins and door surrounds. They also have decorative cast-iron door furniture. Together, the two doors and porches provide good flanking entrances to the attractive building which was commissioned as the village school in 1860 by Louisa, Marchioness of Waterford. We have previously mentioned Lady Waterford's Pre-Raphaelite style paintings that were seen every day by the children until the building closed as a school in 1957.

The right-hand entrance door and porch to the Lady Waterford Hall.

Doors and Windows

Front doors to the churches and older houses in the villages were solidly built, reflecting the need for security but also the fact that they were welcoming points for visitors; they also reflected the status of the house and the occupier. Some of the fairly simple doors to be seen in the villages with their differing styles, are shown below:

a)   b)   c)

d)   e)   f)

Photo a) shows a modern door set into a Tudor style stone surround in Branxton. Photo b) shows the front double doors of the 1932 Art Deco United Reformed Church (previously the English Presbyterian Church) in Crookham which have simple, vertical boarding or paling with decorative iron hinges. Hinges could be of wrought (or worked) iron rather than cast (or moulded) iron as the former stands up better to outside use particularly as the latter tends to be brittle. Photo c) shows the (now) side door of Crookham Village Hall, again with decorative hinges. Photo d) shows a basic ledged and braced door at the rear of the former dairy in Crookham with long, wrought iron hinges which may have been fashioned at the blacksmith's shop which used to be opposite the dairy on the south side of the village street and which was partially excavated by TillVAS in 2016. Photo e) shows an unusual herringbone pattern.

Ledged and braced doors consist of vertical, tongued and grooved boarding on the outside with top, middle and bottom cross battens on the inside. On this inside face (see left), two diagonal 'braces' are fixed between the cross battens to provide more strength to the door. Ledged and braced doors would have been used for back doors, doors to outhouses, doors in garden and boundary walls and doors in agricultural buildings where they would often be two-leaved like those shown on page 77.

Doors and Windows

Arched doorways and openings with granary above at Mardon Farm between Branxton & Crookham.

Unlike the barn door opening shown in photo f) on page 77, the cart/implement sheds at Mardon, above, have segmental stone arches instead of a timber lintel. The stone arch is a stronger as well as a more decorative building structure. Originally the shed doors on the right could have been lockable in order to protect implements. To the left, two bays are now covered by a sliding door and, at the far left, an opening has been rebuilt in concrete block with an RSJ lintel above. Probably the bays to the left would originally have been without doors for housing carts and machinery or used as an open-fronted cattle shed.

Open-fronted bays with granary or hayloft above, at Barelees Farm.

Unlike the stone arches at Mardon which are 'segmental', meaning that the circular arch is less than 180 degrees, the open-fronted bays at Barelees Farm have arches that are more like Tudor 'depressed' arches which rise to a slight point in the middle and look as though they have been flattened under pressure. The arches shown above have projecting 'keystones' and there are other examples in the area which suggests that the same mason was employed on a number of local projects.

Whether segmental or depressed, the curved shape of the arch spreads the load of the arch and the wall above to the springing points on either side and then vertically downwards through the dressed rybats on either side of the opening. The arch is built using a timber former with the 'voussoirs' (the individually shaped arch stones) placed on top. When the central 'keystone' is dropped into place, the timber former can be removed, even without the voussoirs being bedded in mortar. The photo on the left shows another small door at Sandyford Farm, Crookham although the springing stone on the right seems to have lost a portion. Here the dressed springing stones do not rest on similarly dressed rybats but on random rubble that is built roughly to courses to reflect the lesser importance of this particular door.

Windows: In very early times windows would have just been small holes in the wall which might have been covered by material or protective bars or shutters. The origin of 'window' is said to be 'wind eye' from Old Norse *vindauga* from *vindr* 'wind' and *auga* 'eye'.[15] It is difficult to find very early windows or window openings in the four villages that are good examples of their period and have not been altered beyond recognition. The earliest surviving buildings which might contain very early windows (and other features such as doors) are St Paul's Church, Branxton, St. Michael's Church, Ford, Etal Castle and Ford Castle. However, many alterations have occurred over the centuries and the 19th century was particularly renowned for church 'renovations'.

However, if we look at the rear (NW) elevation of the 14th century King James's Tower at Ford Castle, we can be confident that the lower of the four windows (see right and below) survives in its original 14th century form with its small lintel carved to form a narrow, pointed arch above chamfered and rebated rybats. The window needed to be small and narrow for defensive purposes; this one is a vertical arrow slit and not the later cross shape which would allow for a wider line of sight or even use of a crossbow. Another very simple unglazed window can be seen in the wall of an old barn near Branxton, shown on page 6. In that case, the window is small and narrow although not for defensive purposes but just to allow for ventilation with some minimum light.

Fenestration evolved during the 15th, 16th and 17th centuries with mainly fixed windows, perhaps with internal shutters to keep out the draughts, becoming more sophisticated with stone tracery, moulded mullions and deep projecting cills. It wasn't until the 17th century that sliding sash windows were introduced into Britain; originally they would have been single-sash windows sliding horizontally until they were superseded by vertically sliding sashes held in position by wedges or pegs. The invention of the double-sash window sliding vertically is said to have been a British invention but there are counter claims. Many of the traditional or vernacular style buildings still to be seen in the villages and which date from the 18th and 19th centuries have double-hung sash windows, i.e. both the upper and lower windows (the sashes) slid up and down by means of cords and weights, rather than swinging outwards as happens with casement windows. One of the commonest types of window is the 4-pane window (see above) where the upper and lower sashes are divided into two panes and the panes are in similar proportion to the overall window.

The upper sash projects over the lower sash in order to prevent rain penetration. A typical 4-pane window has vertical strips of wood dividing the panes, known as 'muntins' (but as we are in the Borders, the Scottish term of 'astragals' may be heard). The horizontal timber separating the upper and lower sashes is known as the 'transom'. The 4-pane window is perhaps the most traditional design for small, domestic windows in the second half of the 19th century in north Northumberland, Berwickshire, the Lothians and Fife. However there is no hard and fast rule about what is the most traditional design of window in this area and the four villages contain many variations in design. The 4-pane window (page 83) can be dated to the mid or later part of the 19th century because of the 'horns' projecting down from the frame of the upper sash.

The muntins in Georgian or early 19th century windows are usually thinner than those in later windows, giving a more delicate effect. This can be seen to some degree in the photo of the 16-pane window on the left although this window dates from the first year of Queen Victoria's reign, 1837. The overlapping painting of the muntins has disguised their thinness to some extent but the delicacy of the structure is still apparent. There are no 'horns' projecting below the upper sash (see horns in photo on page 83) which is another clue that suggests a date in the earlier part of the 19th century. This example is from the Old Vicarage at Branxton.

There is a wide range of window styles from different eras and some of these are shown here. The first, on the left, is an unpretentious, 19th century six-pane, fixed window set into the wall of one of the old dairy buildings in Crookham, the second, page 85, top left, is a 12-pane window dating from 1912 at Crookham Village Hall and the third, top right, is an Edwardian window in Ford Village, having four 8-pane windows with each section separated by stone mullions.

The 19th century east window of the 12th century Grade II listed St. Paul's Church, Branxton is much more formal with leaded lights and some stained glass, flanking columns with cushion capitals and semi-circular sandstone arches with a drip moulding. The red sandstone arch contrasts well with the surrounding, lighter sandstone.

Romanesque style east window of St. Paul's Church, Branxton

The windows of Crookham Village Hall appear to echo an ecclesiastical style even although the hall was built as a Reading Room in 1912 and not as a church hall. The architect simply chose a Gothic style. It is good to see that the village hall windows have recently been replaced by timber units, rather than the cheaper, non-traditional option of uPVC windows.

Crookham Village Hall, built in 1912.

Window frames should always be set well back from the face of the wall with sufficient 'reveals' on either side and preferably rebated behind the reveals for protection from rain. On older buildings, moulded features were often built in above doors and windows and these have a very practical as well as a decorative purpose. The 'drip' or 'hood' mouldings, seen in the photos on pages 85 and 86, divert rainwater running down the face of the building in order to prevent drips. Note the horizontal 'stop ends' of the drip mouldings above the east window at St. Paul's Church and also at Crookham Village Hall. Also worth noting are the finely carved 'voussoirs' and 'keystone' forming the semi-circular arches at St. Paul's Church.

Instead of plain stop ends, the lancet windows in the south aisle of the 13th century Grade II* listed St. Michael's Church, Ford, have attractive 'headstops' below the Gothic-style drip moulding. These would have been installed during the 1853 renovations.

The head of a lancet window and lancet arch in the south aisle of St. Michael's Church, Ford, showing the drip moulding and headstops.

Old glass can be recognised by its distortion and wavy lines. This might be 'crown glass' or 'cylinder glass'. Crown glass, which was common in the 18th century, although still made through into the 20th century, was manufactured by mouth-blowing a sphere which was then opened out and flattened. This was transferred to the glassmaker's pontil (an iron rod) before being reheated and then rotated at speed to form a large disc. Several panes of glass could be cut out of each disc with the best glass coming from the outer portion of the disc. Crown glass windows were often bowed as a result of a secondary cooling process.

Cylinder glass, commonly used in the 19th century, was mouth-blown into a bottle-shaped cylinder from which the two ends were cut off. The cylinder was then re-heated and unrolled to give a flat piece of glass which was allowed to cool slowly.

Also during the 19th century, large areas of polished plate glass for grander windows were made by casting sheets of glass on to a table and grinding and polishing them by hand. Plate glass was a very flat type of glass but its manufacture was initially an expensive process. In the 20th century, 'drawn sheet glass' was produced by lifting molten glass in sheet form out of a vat and passing it through rollers. Modern glass windows are made of 'float glass', which is made by floating molten glass over a bed of tin. It is very accurate in its dimensions and it can be produced in long lengths. This is now only part of the story because modern glass comes in many specialised forms and varieties of treatment such as laminated glass, toughened glass, coated glass, mirrored glass and patterned glass.

Doors and Windows

As techniques improved during the 19th century it was possible to manufacture larger glass sheets at cheaper cost so that windows did not need to be divided into smaller panes. The windows at Ford Westfield Farmhouse illustrate this very well. Each of the windows only has two large plate glass sash windows probably dating from the middle to later part of the 19th century.

East elevation of Ford Westfield Farmhouse.

Domestic windows and windows on public buildings are not the only ones to be seen in the villages. There are some interesting examples of workshop windows such as this broken window in Crookham which

89

was photographed during building renovation. Fixed windows with no opening lights were commonly used for workshops, mills and smithies in the Borders in the 18th and 19th centuries. Note the stone rybats flanking the window and the stone lintel and cill. The frames and muntins could be of wood or metal (cast iron or zinc) and the often, large windows were designed to admit plenty of light rather than air. The long, vertical muntins hold overlapping panes of glass without horizontal fixing and, originally, the small size of the panes might have been determined by their production from cylinder glass. A practical reason for this might be speculated that if someone or something broke the window in a working environment, it was cheaper and easier to replace one or more small panes rather than a whole window.

Another workshop window can be seen on page 91; this is in the former smithy next to the Bluebell Inn. The window is constructed entirely of metal and is a casement (side-opening) window which would have been a replacement for an earlier window. Early metal windows from the 18th century were made of cast iron but this one is a 20th century window made of steel and is probably a 'Crittall' window (the name of the largest manufacturer to produce relatively cheap and standardised steel windows during the last century). Steel windows, post 1950, would usually have been hot-dip galvanised (with zinc) for protection before painting. Today, metal windows are usually made of aluminium.

Agricultural buildings would not necessarily have had glazed windows where the emphasis was on ventilation. Here is another window from the old dairy in Crookham where the opening has a timber frame and vertical slats to provide a through draught. The lintel is also of wood and the simple cill consists of upright header bricks laid in mortar as is the case with the 6-pane window on page 84.

There is another kind of agricultural window above a former stable and/or carthouse at the Old Vicarage in Branxton. The upper part of the window is glazed but the lower part has unglazed vertical slats with a prominent, stone cill. These two windows are very characteristic of window openings associated with agricultural buildings in the Borders.

Most of the windows (and doors) that we have looked at in previous examples have been surrounded by lintels, cills and rybats. These create straight-sided openings which make it easier to install frames and to avoid draughty gaps around the frames. The photo on the left shows a window in a barn at Sandyford Farm, Crookham, where there are no rybats and it has been necessary to apply cement mortar to create straight sides to the random rubble of the window opening. The small, glazed window has a substantial lintel for its size and we wonder whether it has been reclaimed from somewhere else. There is also a very narrow stone cill in relation to the size of the lintel.

As mentioned earlier, arches and lintels over doors and windows have important structural significance but they also have a decorative role; an opening without a lintel or an arch would not look quite right. The survival of arches and lintels in classical Greek and Roman buildings is a testament to their strength over the centuries and there is no doubt as to their lasting aesthetic appeal. So much so that imitations can occur for purely decorative effect such as the red bricks built into the stonework above the lintels in the Edwardian house in Crookham Village on page 93.

Doors and Windows

Decorative brick arches above stone lintels on an Edwardian house in Crookham Village.

A flat or 'Jack' arch at Ford Westfield Farmhouse.

The flat or 'Jack' arch on page 93 is an example of a straight horizontal arch where the intrados (the bottom edge) is completely flat or only has a slight rise. The extrados (the top edge) is also flat and the keystone is no more prominent than the voussoirs. Although the arch is flat the voussoirs are still mutually supportive but the wedge shapes have to be cut very finely to achieve the required support.

There are so many different styles of windows to see in our area and the two photos below show simple examples of what can be very elaborate styles. The opening in the belfry at St. Paul's Church, Branxton, is built in the 11th and 12th century Romanesque style which developed before the advent of Gothic style and was derived from the architecture of ancient Rome. In England, Romanesque is a style also referred to as

Belfry, St. Paul's Church, Branxton   **King James's Tower (SW), Ford.**

'Norman' because it was introduced here after the Norman conquest of 1066 AD. The rounded arches and supporting columns are solid and strong and this is also reflected in the rounded vaults and arches to be seen inside Norman castles and cathedrals. The Romanesque style contrasts with Greek architecture which does not use vaults or arches and also with the Gothic style which followed the Romanesque and which features pointed arches above doors and windows.

The Gothic style introduced window 'tracery' and the windows on the side (SW) elevation of the King James's Tower at Ford Castle, although they are not original, show a simple stone 'Y tracery' where the central stone mullion branches into two to enclose the space created at the point of the arch. More elaborate forms of tracery developed as Gothic windows became wider, resulting in the many geometrical shapes with circles and trefoils to be seen, for example, in English cathedrals from the late 13th century onwards. Later, vertical tracery became popular within long, narrow windows of the perpendicular style of the 14th century.

5
Roofs

When walking around the villages, it is worth looking up at the varied roofs and roof lines of the old and new buildings, taking care not to be crossing the road at the same time! Also, when viewing farmhouses and farm buildings from the road (or closer to, with the owner's permission), have a look at the materials on the roofs and consider the practical reasons for their use. The difference in height and type of roof along a long-established street frontage is one of the reasons why old buildings can have such an appeal, compared with more modern and more uniform buildings.

Interesting roof lines are more apparent where there are buildings of different height and design within a terraced street but there can be plenty of variety in height, structure and materials in a village streetscape with a mixed development that has evolved over the years. This is helped where there are materials of different colours and textures and different roof styles and features. There may be slates, pantiles, corrugated iron or thatch, stone or brick chimney-stacks, differently shaped chimney pots, dormer windows, porch roofs and roof slopes of different angles and styles. We will look at examples of these in the next few pages.

In the 18th century and before, roofs in this area would have been covered by straw, reed, heather or turf thatch but these were mostly superseded by non-combustible slates or by clay tiles during the 19th century. However, thatch remained as a roof covering in Etal Village into the early 20th century and can still be seen on a few buildings to the present day. During the 19th century, the attractive but primitive cottages in Etal were occupied by estate workers and tradespeople who leased their cottages from the then Etal Estate. After the Etal Estate was purchased by the 1st Baron Joicey in 1908, improvements to the village took place during the early part of the 20th century. The cottages were replaced on both sides of the village street by houses and cottages with slated roofs except for two of the new cottages that have thatched roofs.

Houses that remain from earlier times are the old cottages near the former mill and the former parsonage (see page 42). Most of the cottages retain the characteristic white walls and those that do not, have dressed sandstone walls. Today the recently renovated Black Bull remains the only thatched public house in Northumberland. The life expectancy of thatch is ten to fifteen years for ridge thatch, fifteen to twenty-five for long straw, twenty-five to thirty-five for combed wheat reed and twenty-five to forty years or more for water reed. Long straw is cultivated uncombed reed of up to three feet; combed wheat reed is cut young, soft but durable, producing rounded hips and curved eaves; water reed is longer and harder, survives longer and produces more angular or straight edges. The top photo on page 98 shows the Black Bull before the village improvements. The bottom photo shows the westernmost wing of the public house, today. One adjoining cottage, and part of another, may have been retained when the other cottages were demolished and were then incorporated within the Black Bull. Speculation is something that can be enjoyed when studying old buildings.

Aspects of Buildings and Monuments: Branxton, Crookham, Etal, Ford

The Black Bull, early 20th century.   **Old postcard in authors' collection.**

The left-hand wing of The Black Bull—part of the former cottage, above left.

Being close to the Scottish border, thick and chunky Scottish slates, like the ones shown below, were often used in the villages. They might have come from elsewhere in the Borders such as the Peebles area or from the West Highlands, such as the deep, blue-black slates from Ballachulish in Lochaber or perhaps they might be midnight-blue slates from the Glens of Foudland in Aberdeenshire. Texture, thickness and colour cause variations making it difficult to identify the source. Scottish slates are said to have been used on the wings of Pallinsburn House and at the Old Vicarage at Branxton. Other slates may have come from quarries in England such as the green and grey Westmorland slates on the roof of the chapel of St. Mary the Virgin at Etal or the patterned, green Lakeland and grey Welsh slates on the roof of the Lady Waterford Hall in Ford as seen on page 100.

During the 19th century, the predominant slate used in the villages was Welsh slate which was plentiful, thin, easy to split and yet possessed qualities of durability and impermeability. Welsh slate came from many quarries throughout the Principality and in many different blue-grey colours, but a popular slate was the 'Bangor Blue' which came from a long-running quarry (some 400 years or so) in Bethesda in North Wales. From the 1980s, the use of Welsh slate has been overtaken by imported Spanish slate which is geologically younger and, many would say, inferior in quality. These slates have a smoother, less traditional look to them which, in our view, does not sit comfortably on older buildings.

A section of the patterned and differently coloured slate roof at the Lady Waterford Hall, Ford.

Because the four villages are so close to the Scottish Border, there has been inevitably some overlapping of building techniques but, generally, practices have been firmly embedded in Northumberland and English traditions. However, it is interesting to be aware of differing techniques. In relation to slate fixing, the traditional method in Scotland was always to 'head nail' with one nail through the top of the slate on to flat boarding or 'sarking' with the horizontal boards butted together, as opposed to the English method of slate fixing with two nails at the top of the slate on to lath strips. The use of sarking boards in Scotland provided more insulation but the single nail meant that the slates were susceptible to sideways movement and to being lifted by the wind. However, if Scottish slates were used, their weight counteracted this with the advantage that the slates could more easily be swung aside on their single nail for replacement of other, damaged slates. The Scottish climate, and perhaps that of north Northumberland, dictates a roof slope of at least forty degrees for quicker run-off of rainwater and discharge of snow.

The very best practice in the 19th century, usually only reserved for special buildings, was to use a system of graduated or diminishing slate courses with the largest and heaviest slates at the bottom of the roof slope where they were best placed to withstand weathering and the greater flow of rainwater and where their weight would be directly transferred to the wall. As the slater moved up the slope, the slates would decrease in size, row by row with the smallest slates near the ridge as is the case at Etal Peace Memorial Hall, shown here. As well as having a practical function, the graduated style has a pleasing effect. The slates on the

Memorial Hall are unusual, being very large, green and chunky (far more so than the Scottish slates shown on page 99). When the hall was opened in 1926, the slates were described as 'green Welsh slate slabs'.[16] Their size and thickness do not equate with the usual image of Welsh slates and they must have been a special order from a particular quarry. They have a very attractive appearance and their use was repeated in the two adjoining cottages at the entrance to the village.

Slate roofs of all kinds could be capped by a lead or zinc flashing or, better still, by clay ridge tiles which, during the 19th century or in later imitations, often had moulded scallops or other decorative treatment. Dormer and porch roofs might have similar decorative ridges with clay, timber or iron finials. This post-19th example (but without finials) is on a porch at the Blue Row, Branxton. Again, note the thinner, Welsh slates compared with the Scottish slates shown on page 99.

Another type of roof covering to be seen in this area is the red-clay pantiled roof with triangular, third or half-round ridge tiles. Pantiles are particularly associated with east-central Scotland, the Lothians, Fife and eastern England. They are thought to have originated as ballast in the empty holds of trading vessels returning to Britain from northern Europe.

Instead of dumping the usual ballast, the alternative ballast of pantiles provided a cheap and plentiful supply of roofing material. The popularity of pantiles led to their manufacture in England and Scotland and the fact that they were often made locally could also make them cheaper than slates. Perhaps the nearest tile works was the Flodden Brick and Tileworks alongside the present A697 road, south of the junction with the present B6354 road, as previously mentioned on page 64. The Works were said to have been established in 1768 by Lord Delaval, during improvements to the Ford Estate. The Works provided bricks, plain tiles and pantiles for the Estate and beyond. By 1771, it is said that 100,000 bricks were being produced each year with the same number of pantiles. The site was later used from 1860 to 1902 to produce a number of articles other than bricks and tiles.[17]

The colour of pantiles (generally, not just at Flodden Brick & Tileworks) varied from orange through red to black, depending upon the origin of the clay. Over time, the pantiles weathered and developed a patina as well as attracting lichens which add to their appearance. Unlike slates, pantiles were not nailed down. Instead, generous applications of lime mortar (known as 'torching') were applied on the underside of the tiles to keep them in place; later, nibs were moulded on the tiles' top edges and these were hooked over timber battens that were nailed to the rafters. Pantiles overlapped the row below and also overlapped laterally but the single lapping and curly 'S' profile meant that roof spaces could be very draughty compared with slate-covered roofs despite liberal amounts of torching underneath. The dilapidated outhouse roof at Crookham, on the left, gives some idea of the overlapping tiles, battens and rafters. There are no remains of torching, perhaps because the tiles were adequately held in place by nibs and because draught-proofing was not important for an outhouse. In some areas, it was common practice to lay two or three rows of slates above the eaves so that the flat slates could cut out the draughts blowing up under the pantiles. A similar effect can be seen at the old chicken shed at Heatherslaw Mill (see above), where a concrete tile course has been laid at eaves level. Some

torching can just be seen protruding from the bottom pantile course. Like slate roofs, pantiled roofs would usually have clay ridge-tiles bedded in lime mortar and these would vary in their profile.

Modern concrete and clay machine-made tiles can be seen in the villages as replacements on old roofs or as roof coverings on new buildings. They are regular in size and do not have the variation in shape and colour of hand-made tiles. They can be single-lap pantiles as seen in the photos on pages 103/104 or they can be double-lap tiles, known as Roman tiles. Even machine-made tiles will weather eventually and attract lichen as can be seen with the plain clay tiles seen above left, but they will never have the same character. However, they are practical and cheaper than hand-made tiles.

Contrast their plainness with the fish-scale tiles or slates on the roof of the Grade II-listed game larder at Ford Castle built in the 19th century for the Marchioness of Waterford.

There are also examples in the villages of roof coverings made of asbestos-cement tiles such as the red tiles at Crookham Village Hall, and the corrugated, asbestos-cement sheeting on an outhouse at Laburnam Cottage, Crookham. Asbestos is a naturally occurring silicate

Asbestos-cement tiles, above. Corrugated asbestos sheeting, below.

and its worldwide use goes back at least 4,500 years although, in Britain, its combination with Portland cement to form asbestos-cement sheeting for building only became popular at the beginning of the 20th century.

If asbestos-cement roof coverings are in good condition, there is no risk to health as the asbestos fibres are embedded in the cement and the material has a long life-span. There is only a risk if the material becomes damaged, when the fibres could be released into the air and into people's lungs, possibly causing asbestosis. Dismantling or disposal of asbestos-cement needs to be carried out with care, preferably by handling whole sheets rather than breaking them into pieces.

Asbestos-cement has been a very useful building material over the years because it does not corrode and is fireproof although fibres can be released as a result of heat damage. It has good insulating properties and was used not just for roofing but for internal insulation panels, ceiling tiles, pipe lagging, rainwater gutters and downpipes. But it is brittle and there is the health risk mentioned above. There is legislation in place that bans the import and use of most asbestos products and there are guidelines regulating the management of already existing products. Comprehensive guidance notes cover the latest regulations and the methods of disposal including protective wear. Work involving asbestos materials defined as being on a medium to large scale, including removal and demolition or where asbestos insulation cannot be removed without being broken, needs a licence issued by the Health & Safety Executive.

Traditional roof coverings also include corrugated iron which should not be dismissed as a sub-standard, cheap and an easy alternative to other forms of roofing materials. It does not have the health risks of asbestos-cement, and it has a longer history of use in Britain having been invented here in the 1820s. Corrugated iron, which was pressed into shape by fluted rollers, developed further during the 1830s with a process of protecting the iron with a zinc coating (galvanizing) so that, by the 1840s, several manufacturers were producing it for roofing and even for wall cladding. Because it was lightweight with each sheet having a large expanse, it could be fixed directly on to timber roof frames with less support. Its light weight and quickness of construction meant that it could easily be shipped overseas to meet the requirements of colonial expansion.

In Britain, corrugated iron was ideal for covering large areas on

Corrugated iron roof covering on an old workshop in Branxton.

farm buildings and it could also be placed on top of domestic thatch, so avoiding rethatching whilst retaining its insulating properties. Waterproofing was obtained by overlapping sheets by two or three corrugations, laterally, and by six inches or so, vertically. Wrought iron gave way to galvanized mild steel by the end of the 19th century although it was often still referred to as corrugated iron. In the photo on page 108, note the mixture of materials that clad the building.

Another example of corrugated iron can just be seen from the road in Branxton. This is the old 'Tin Tabernacle', now standing in a private garden but, at one time, a Primitive Methodist chapel that was still in use in 1940 some eight years after the Primitive Methodists united with other branches to form the present Methodist Church.[18] The building was

A glimpse of the 'Tin Tabernacle' Branxton seen from the public highway.

clad entirely of corrugated iron fixed by nails to a timber frame and was bought as a kit from a catalogue, either for self-assembly or for delivery and erection by the seller. Prefabricated corrugated iron buildings had been exhibited at the Great Exhibition of 1851 and became very popular during the last half of the 19th century for use, for example, as churches, cottages, railway stations and houses. They were lightweight, strong and cheap, costing from £150 for a chapel seating 150 people to say, £500 for a church seating 350 people.[19]

The 'Tin Tabernacle', Branxton, erected 1897.   Photo, TillVAS archives.

The only decorative features to be seen on the chapel are the painted, shaped fascia boards whereas, elsewhere, the chapels and churches received embellishments such as Gothic spires and bell-towers.

Roofs

Today there are many other metallic forms of 'corrugated iron' such as profiled aluminium, zinc and copper which are regarded as high quality roofing materials, for example in Australia and the USA.

Roof slopes, whether of slate, tile or other material, may extend over the gable ends of a building, but often the gables would be built up above roof height to form a sloping upstand or gable parapet (known in Scotland as a 'skew'). The gable parapet is usually topped by flat coping stones known as 'tabling'. Gable parapets can be quite plain as can be seen, left, in this simple example on the roof of the outhouse in Crookham described previously on page 104. The lowest stone, the 'kneeler' (or in Scotland, the 'skewputt'), is usually larger and shaped, in order to transfer the load on to the quoins. In this case, the extra-large quoin below the kneeler has also been shaped either for decorative or utilitarian purposes. Sometimes, the kneeler is decorated with a carved scroll or, in the case of the photo of the Schoolmaster's House at Crookham, top left on page 112, a stone finial. In the photo of a house in Branxton, top right on page 112, there is a plain kneeler and an 'S' profile quoin below.

111

Where slates or tiles abutted a raised gable parapet or the wall of another building, traditionally the junction between the roof slope and the wall would be sealed by a lead 'flashing' or a mortar 'fillet'. Other materials that have come into use include zinc, copper, zinc-coated lead and stainless steel. In the example, top right, the junction has been sealed with a metallic, possibly zinc, flashing. For a junction such as this one between a pantiled roof and a stone gable, a mortar joint would have been the most common method used in the past in order to adequately seal the gaps at the end of the pantiles.

There are all kinds of decorative features to be seen in the villages that can often be missed by the casual observer. This is a stone projection at the apex of the roof next to the pantiled roof in the photo, top right. This feature can be seen on a number of buildings in the area, so the same mason must have been employed, one who had his own 'signature' design.

Chimney stacks consist of three elements, the plinth rising from the roof, the shaft, and the cornice. The chimney pot or pots ('cans' in Scotland) are placed above the cornice (and the chimney flue) and are usually embedded in a waterproof cement or mortar capping known as 'flaunching'. The pot or pots sit above one or more flues which serve separate fireplaces, often on different floors. The pots increase the draw on the chimney, making for better burning of fuel in the fireplaces below, as well as deflecting smoke away from the building. The photo on the right shows a 19th century sandstone chimney stack on the gable end of a house in Crookham. It displays the three elements and, in this case, the shaft has two projecting decorative bands above the wider plinth and the cornice is staggered outwards. The shaft is also 'waisted' and the overall effect is quite unusual. It can be seen that the whole of the stonework is blackened from the effect of hot, acidic fumes from internal coal fires penetrating the stonework or from smoke generated by the many chimneys in the area before the advent of smokeless fuels following the Clean Air Act 1956. This is not surprising as, given the rapid expansion of coal mining in the area, coal became the predominant fuel in north Northumberland from the 17th century onwards.

Because the sulphates in coal can have such an impact on the structure of sandstone, it became common practice to build the shaft and cornice in brickwork as brick itself, being a fired material, can withstand heat and fumes. The chimney on the left retains the stone plinth but the shaft and the cornice are of brick. There are many examples of this form of construction across the Borders with differently coloured bricks frequently determined by their source and often chosen in order to tone in with the stonework. The three chimney pots above service three flues and these would be lined internally with lime or mortar render or 'parging' to prevent gases escaping through mortar joints or cracks in the structure. The parging would usually be of the same mix as the brickwork mortar as it would be applied at the same time as the chimney building. Special mixes were used in older buildings to include ox hair or cow dung. Lime mortar is acknowledged to be more resistant to heat and fumes than cement mortar but Building Regulations now require all new chimney flues to have approved flue liners determined by the type of combustible fuel.

Unlike the chimney stacks on pages 113 and 114, that shown on the left is not sited at the gable end; it also has a taller cornice than the previous examples. The stack probably needed additional height in its position at the bottom of the roof slope in order to create sufficient draw. The second photo, below, shows a squatter stack with a short, brick and stone cornice; there is no plinth and the brickwork is built directly above the roof slopes and ridge. Cement mortar fillets can be seen at the junction between the ridge, stack, slates, and gable parapet.

The photo below shows a chimney stack with traditional plinth, shaft and cornice except that the plinth and the top course of the cornice are in concrete. Note the decorative dentilation below the cornice, the stone 'ball' finial topping the gable parapets on the dormer roof, the terracotta ridge tiles and the Welsh slates.

The earliest chimney stacks in England were probably to be found in castles from around the 12th century and they would not have been capped by chimney pots. Chimney stacks did not come into widespread use until the 16th century when they ranged between simple, utilitarian examples and highly ornate examples of the Tudor period with their spirals, chevrons and other decorative features. There is still a wide variety of interesting chimney stacks in our area but few highly ornamental ones. Chimney pots have probably been in use in England since the 13th century when it was realized that they were efficient in funnelling billowing smoke and improved the draw. Draw can be increased by cowls above the pots and rigid, stainless steel liners between stoves and chimney pots have led to increased efficiency and prevented internal chemical damage to flues.

Chimney pots come in many shapes, sizes and materials and there are still hundreds of designs available on the market. Although materials now include copper and stainless steel, the traditional material is clay. This has three main finishes, terracotta red, terracotta buff and salt glaze (a ceramic glaze created by throwing salt into the kiln at the highest firing point to create extra weatherproofing and extended life for the pot). Terracotta comes from the Latin for 'baked or cooked earth' and refers to any clay that changes colour during firing to anything between dull ochre and red but also including rare colour finishes. High quality pots are still made by hand for prestige work such as restoration work on listed buildings but standard clay pots are machine-made. Hand-made and machine-made clay pots were made in vast numbers during the 19th century. The two moulded-clay pots on the left, seen in Crookham, show that function was not the only consideration and that much thought went into the design. It is not surprising that antique, decorative pots are much sought after in reclamation yards, for use as planters.

The photo, below left, shows an unusual 19th century chimney pot from Staffordshire used as a planter in a garden in Etal. Chimney pots are works of art and can be cylindrical or rectangular such as the pot in the photo. They can be louvred, thus incorporating the benefits of a built-in cowl or they can have particular ornamentation such as the 'crown top' pot. Chimney pots are even a reasonably affordable way of customizing houses and a BBC feature on the Stoke & Staffordshire Chimney Pot Museum has a link to a chimney 'spotter's' list with drawings of 112 pots. Many of these have exotic names such as the 'Octagonal Twist Captain' and the 'Square Panelled Taper Lift'.[20]

The photograph of Ford Westfield Farmhouse on page 89 shows four crown top chimney pots but, because they are at a distance, they are difficult to see in detail. Two pots of identical design, shown here, can be seen at the interesting Hirsel Homestead museum near Coldstream.

Here is an unusual pair of chimney pots in Crookham Village that now provide outlets for a modern flue system. Each pot is formed from two cast, concrete halves, cemented together. They give the impression of concrete made with pumice aggregate which, if also used for the flue liners below, would give much better insulation. Even if they are just textured concrete, the pots are decorative and sit happily above the slate-covered roof.

From the beginning of the 19th century, the mass production of cast iron gutters and rainwater downpipes (rhones or rones in Scotland) meant that these could be fitted to all buildings, (except for thatch). Cast iron goods could be easily sourced in the north of England which helped to keep the cost down. Cast iron is very tough in compression but is brittle in tension and cannot withstand heavy knocks. It is very hardwearing and gutters can take heavy snow deposits without bending and buckling like PVC guttering. It does, however, require regular painting, unlike PVC or uPVC, in order to prevent rusting. The casting process allowed for quite elaborate profiles and decorations on gutters, downpipes, brackets and on the 'hopper-heads' at the top of the downpipes that received rainwater from the gutters. Standard gutters had a half-round profile with circular-section down pipes as shown below.

A standard 4.5 inch, half-round gutter and circular downpipe, both painted and in good condition on a house in Crookham Village.

The photo also shows the effect of the painted exposed rafter ends behind the gutter and the painted inverted 'V' shaped, moulded fascia boards at the end of the main roof (abutting the chimney stack and above the gable). The dressed stone quoins and the dressed stone chimney stack, can also be seen contrasting with the squared, rubble walls. The main roof covering is Welsh slate whereas the roof below is covered in concrete tiles. Where roof slopes meet walls and chimney stack, zinc flashings have been used, sealed with mortar. The gutter discharges into the downpipe without a collecting hopper-head.

Historic hopper-heads were often very elaborate and displayed the craftsman's art. They were made in cast iron or lead as in the following example from Pallinsburn House which displays columns, scrolls, the initials of the then owner, Major Charles Mitchell and, although difficult to spot, the date 1911. This impressive, lead hopper-head is therefore not as old as it looks but it reflects the Jacobean or even Jacobethan style of the remodeling of the house that was carried out by Major Mitchell. It would be hard to find other examples that surpass the hopper-heads at Pallinsburn House, even on Jacobean mansions.

An elaborate, lead hopper-head at Pallinsburn House. The initials CM are in the centre with 19 within the scrolls on the left and 11 within those on the right.

Normally, gutters were, and are, fixed to the fascia boards under the eaves of the roof slope or, as in the case of the roof on page 120, to the projecting ends of the rafters. However, for what is known as a 'one and a half storey house' or a 'two and a half storey house' (meaning that the upper storey lies partly within the roof space), any dormers would interrupt the eaves gutters. The best solution would be to have 'stop-ends' on the gutters on either side of the dormers with additional downpipes as necessary, as in the example below.

Roof of a house with dormers in Branxton and three downpipes.

Alternatively, the gutter could be carried across the front of the dormer, as in another example in Branxton. This second solution seems very strange and architecturally undesirable but it is one that is often seen in parts of Scotland and seems to have been adopted to some extent in north Northumberland. This is understandable where property professionals and trades operated on both sides of the Border. The 'gutter across window' style can be seen in the photo on the right. Older buildings that were thatched, or even those with pantiled roofs, would not have had gutters and the rainwater would have dripped from the overhanging eaves.

There are many styles of roof to be seen across the north of England and the Borders but we can only mention a few of them here. The simplest roof style is the pitched, 'gable' roof, the profile of which is an inverted 'V' shape like the cottage roofs at Heatherslaw, shown below. These roofs do not overlap the gables but have stone gable parapets.

Estate Cottages near Heatherslaw Mill.

The cottages show the simplicity of gable roofs with chimney stacks at either end of each cottage. These Ford Estate cottages are shown on the First Edition of the Ordnance Survey map, surveyed in 1860, and could have been occupied by agricultural workers or workers at Heatherslaw Mill. The majority of workers at Forge Ford on the other side of the river would probably have lived near the forge spadeworks erected in 1769.[21] The 1861 census for Heatherslaw Mill does list three blacksmiths but these are aged 15 and 16 years and it is possible that they were apprentices at the Ford Spade works; they would have had to cross the river by the footbridge upstream from the present Grade II listed, cast iron, steel and stone bridge which was built in 1877. Apart from the millers at Heatherslaw Mill, male employment listed in the 1861 census includes shoemakers, a stone mason, agricultural labourers and a carter.

We have mentioned the use of decorative bands of green and blue roof slates such as those on the Lady Waterford Hall (see page 100) and there are a number of examples to be seen in Crookham and Ford on buildings constructed during the life interest in the Ford Estate by Louisa, Marchioness of Waterford (1818-1891) after the death of her husband in 1859. The influence of the Marchioness is to be seen in the sometimes elaborate, even quirky, designs of the buildings in Crookham and Ford.

As regards 'add-on' features, the four villages do not, for example, have elaborate, pierced, barge boards on the gable ends although there was a small example at the 'Tin Tabernacle' at Branxton. There is an attractive feature on a cottage in Crookham which has a roof covering in restrained bands of green and blue/grey clay tiles and which has an unusual 'billet frieze' below the gutter. Pevsner describes a billet frieze as meaning, literally, a log or block, and as being a Norman ornament consisting of small half-cylindrical or rectangular blocks placed at regular intervals.[22] The billets can be staggered in alternate rows but the Crookham example has one row with the billets separated by vertical ovolo mouldings as seen in this photo. The sandstone frieze has veins running through it of different colours including brown, grey and honey; these colours are also present in the lintels and rybats of the windows.

A billet frieze in Crookham next to a sandstone gable parapet and kneeler.

Another, common type of roof is the 'hipped' roof ('piended' in Scotland) where the vertical gable roof is replaced by a slope which comes to a point at the ridge as in the example on page 126 showing the Manor Lodge at Etal. The lodge is not shown on the Ordnance Survey map of 1860 but is shown on the map of 1897 and would therefore have been built during Sir James Laing's ownership of the Etal Estate.

All four sides of the roof slope towards the ridge and the chimneys. In theory, a hipped roof is sturdier in high winds and snowy conditions compared with a gable roof but is more expensive to build because of the greater complexity of design. It is worth noting the exposed rafters and the profiles of the sandstone chimney stacks and, straying from roofs for a moment, the raised ashlar quoins and rybats.

Also digressing, there are two bay windows; these were introduced as early as the 16th century but they became popular in the late 19th century and early 20th century. Full height bay windows, as opposed to oriel windows supported by brackets or corbels, needed to be supported on foundations. Bay windows increased the floor area of a room and, particularly in the case of a canted bay (flat front and angled sides) such as those shown below, increased the amount of light flooding into the room and provided additional views of the outside.

Manor Lodge, Etal.

Apart from the pitched, gabled and hipped roof shapes already mentioned, there are a few other basic shapes to be seen in the villages. These include the mono-pitched or 'shed' roof and the flat roof. An example of the shed roof is shown here, being a single-pitched, slated roof which would traditionally have had a lime-mortar fillet between the roof and the gable behind. This particular roof at The Well House, Branxton, is not to be dismissed as an inferior roof; it does not cover a garden shed or an outbuilding although it may cover a utility area in the house. It is flanked by good quality sandstone gable parapets and the whinstone wall beneath has ashlar quoins and ashlar rybats and lintel.

In warmer climates, flat roofs have been used for hundreds, if not thousands of years, built of stone or clay in, for example, Greece and the Middle East. This style continues to the present day in such climates but often using concrete instead of traditional materials. In England and elsewhere in Europe, completely flat roofs only came into widespread use in the 19th century with better waterproof coverings. There had been areas of flat roofing before that, say, in wide valley gutters or other sections on cathedral and church roofs during the early, middle and late medieval periods. Then, the flat sections were covered in lead. From the 19th century, flat roofs have been covered in many materials including lead, copper, zinc, asphalt, galvanized steel, asphalt, fibreglass and rubber. The use of mineral felt in the 1950s proved to be an unreliable and short-lived solution. Probably the largest flat roof area (but not easily seen) in our area is at Pallinsburn House where the main block has a concrete roof hidden behind parapets. The roof was laid when the top storey (see page 127) was removed in around 1933.

There are many other roof profiles in addition to the gable roofs, hipped roofs, shed roofs and flat roofs to be seen elsewhere. However, these are only mentioned in passing as they are found more often in urban settings and do not appear in our rural area. There is the 'mansard' roof (see an example in Coldstream, left) which is distinguishable from a gable roof by having a flat section at the top between the two, pitched slopes. Mansard roofs appear on 19th century houses and are sometimes difficult to see because the flat surface is hidden from ground level unless seen gable-end on.

Where there is a symmetrical, two-sided roof with two slopes on either side and with the top slopes having shallower angles than the lower slopes, this is known as a 'gambrel' roof. It is more common on the

Roofs

continent of Europe and is sometimes called a 'Dutch gambrel' roof (see left). By contrast, a symmetrical roof where the upper slopes are steeper than the lower slopes, such as the combined roof of the nave and south aisle at the Church of St. Michael & All Angels, Ford, shown below, is not a Dutch gambrel.

Church of St. Michael and All Angels, Ford, seen from the south-east.

There are so many things to look out for at roof level like the two-tier bell-cote in the photo above. There are cowls, ventilators, ridge tiles, carvings, mouldings, finials, brackets, wind vanes and so much else in many materials, shapes and sizes. It is worth craning the neck even if this attracts strange glances from passers-by.

129

6
Bits and Pieces

This chapter is headed 'Bits and Pieces' because we are going to be dotting around a bit. At the end of the last chapter, we referred briefly to the many interesting things to be seen at roof level but this comment can apply at all levels of a building and to its surroundings. We will therefore be looking at some of the 'extras' which add to the appearance of buildings or which are interesting in functional terms. It is also worth observing items that are part of the street scene and which attract attention because of their aesthetic or practical interest. Firstly, however, we consider how we might approach the dating of a building.

Dating a building: The first step is to examine any documentary evidence that may be available, because historic documents such as wills, title deeds, tithe maps, early Ordnance Survey maps and old photographs might pinpoint the date of construction or show that a building was not in existence on a certain date. One of the problems is that buildings are usually altered, added to, partially demolished or completely re-clad over the years and it will therefore be necessary to work out the dates of the different phases from the documentary evidence.

Apart from castles and churches, most buildings that we see in and around the villages today only originate from the 19th century and later, although there are notable examples from the 18th century. This is because earlier and more primitive buildings, both domestic and agricultural, were often built of earth, clay and/or timber and thatched with straw or heather; they were often demolished and rebuilt to reflect changing lifestyles caused by such things as the 18th century enclosures of land, better farming practices and greater expectations. Having said that, even though a building looks as though it is 19th century in construction, it might have been built around a surviving 'core' from a much earlier age. This is where the documentary evidence can be of such help in tracing historical changes.

In chapter 2, we looked at some building styles but we were only able to give a limited number of examples. Recognition of style is the second step in determining date although this can be deceptive if, say, a 20th century building has been built in Jacobethan style such as the main building of Pallinsburn House. There are many books about architectural styles and, for Northumberland, the introductory chapters in Pevsner's *Northumberland* provide a concise but detailed description of design and changes in design from prehistoric times up to the twentieth century.[23] Experience counts and, again, documentary evidence, if available, can confirm or deny the initial, visual evidence for a particular building.

The third step in dating is to determine the type of materials used in construction and to examine their appearance. With regard to stone buildings, we can have a look at the quoins, as it is the wall arrises (corner edges) that receive the most weathering and give an indication of age. In the photo on page 132, the quoins on The Manse at Crookham show some weathering. The manse dates from 1750 but, apart from saying that the weathered quoins suggest that it is a building older than the 20th century, it is difficult to be any more precise from this evidence alone. There is some original lime mortar pointing on the stonework to the right of the quoins with later cement mortar repair. Old lime mortar will suggest an older building compared with a building with cement mortar but, in the latter case, it may just be that the 'wrong' sort of mortar has been used in repointing. The stonework to the right of the quoins is also well weathered; some of it shows signs of original stugging but, if so, this has become very worn. Weathering will be greater anyway on a south-west wall angle (as this is) as a result of more rain from the prevailing winds.

As to other changes over time, different-sized stones or a different tone or colour for stone above a certain height will indicate that the upper part of a wall was built at a later date. This might also be true of later additions to the main building. If header and stretcher bricks are used in the same course of brickwork, then this is an indication of a solid wall built before cavity walls were introduced prior to the Second World War. Old-looking bricks of non-standard size (the old imperial standard being 8½ins. by 4ins. by 3½ins.) would indicate a building from before the 19th century. Similarly, hand-made bricks with more irregular lines would indicate an older building compared with factory-pressed bricks on modern buildings.

If the windows look original with 'wavy' glass, this might indicate an 18th century or an early 19th century date. If the muntins are very narrow and there are 12 or 16 or 18 window panes, then this could suggest an 18th century date but it is dangerous to make a pronouncement based on just a few features. Door and fanlight styles may help but doors may have been replaced and so may the windows. Hopefully, if doors and windows have been changed, they will have been replaced as near as possible in the original style. An 18th century stone house, with a 21st century plastic front door, gives a jarring effect. Canted bay windows might suggest a late 19th century building.

Other materials can give a good clue. Lead gutters, hoppers and downpipes might indicate a pre-18th century building (although this would not be the case at Pallinsburn House), whereas cast iron rainwater goods would suggest a 19th century building, or later. Corrugated iron or corrugated asbestos sheets would not have been used before the 19th century but they may have been replacements or they may cover an earlier thatched roof which could still be in place underneath. However, corrugated iron above thatch may not survive in this area unlike, for example, in Devon and Dorset. However, a steeply pitched roof of pantiles or slates might indicate that the original roof covering was in thatch because thatch needs a steeper pitch to prevent rainwater penetration.

The very few examples mentioned above can only be a start to decodifying the age of a building. If we take a straightforward example from Crookham, we know that the former Presbyterian church (now the United Reformed Church, see left) was rebuilt in 1932/33 because there is documentary evidence in the form of church records and contemporary newspaper reports. There is also an inscription plaque above the front door and a dated foundation stone. But if there were no such evidence, we would still know that this was a building dating from the 1930s.

The angled joints of the quoins and random, dressed stone facing, the 'blocky' parapets and the slight Egyptian feel, all suggest an Art Deco style. The shape of the window with its smooth recessed arches above the front door, the narrow 'slit' windows with their plain lintels and cills and the lack of ornamentation all suggest an overall look of the 1930s (see above).

Additional features: Turning now to the 'extras' which we mentioned at the beginning of this chapter. Some of those to be noted are 'stand-alone' features whilst others are attached to a building. None of them come within a dictionary description of a building as 'a structure with walls and a roof, such as a house or factory'.[24] They may still come within the legal definition of a building, perhaps for planning purposes even if they do not have a roof or walls. Definitions do not really matter and included here are examples that are interesting and worth looking at more closely. Some features are often taken for granted with not many people stopping to examine them. Familiarity means that, even if they are noticed, they do not attract any interest.

Buildings and boundaries are always enhanced by the appropriate use of cast and wrought iron for railings, gates, lamp brackets, finials and other ornamental decoration. We did not find many examples in the villages or on the farms, and the use of cast and wrought iron may be more common in towns where, for example, railings were needed around basement 'wells' or to separate townhouses from pavements and streets. There may have been more examples of railings in the villages before the Second World War when there was a large-scale removal for recycling into munitions as a result of a national appeal by the Minister of Aircraft Production, Lord Beaverbrook. There has been much discussion on whether the railings were ever used for recycling or just buried in landfill or dumped at sea.[25] Secrecy seems to surround the answer but, whatever happened, the exercise was probably a morale boosting exercise if people thought that this was helping the war effort.

There are some ornate examples of iron gates still to be seen, such as the Grade II listed gates to the avenue at Etal Manor, illustrated on page 14, the Grade II listed gates at Ford Church, below left, and the Grade II listed garden gates north-west of Pallinsburn House, below right. There is no doubt that wrought iron gates add to the appearance of a property and the lower photo on page 17 shows this in relation to East Lodge, Pallinsburn House in the early 19th century.

Railings with alternate barley twist balusters still survive at Ford Church, (see left), and it is worth seeking out other examples in the villages and also looking for old iron fence posts that once formed part of field boundaries. There is a lone, cast iron survivor in a field at Etal, probably dating to the 19th century. It is next to the road going down to the ford and stands next to a Horse Chestnut tree near the site of an old cottage (see below). Even such a utilitarian object as this, is an interesting product of 19th century design.

Cast iron and wrought iron differ from each other in their composition and method of manufacture. Cast iron is smelted quickly at high temperatures and contains more impurities than wrought iron and it has a higher carbon content than wrought iron. Because of this, it is more prone to rusting and is also hard and brittle, so will break quite easily if struck by, say, a hammer. Wrought iron is a purer form of iron and is smelted more slowly at a lower temperature in order to remove the impurities, meaning that it is softer and can literally be 'wrought' or worked into shape using tools. It is less hard than cast iron but it is still tough, yet malleable, and is therefore useful for bending into intricate shapes. It can also be welded, which is not possible with cast iron.

Cast iron products often reveal the join between their different parts. A good example is down both sides of a rainwater downpipe which is cast in two semicircular lengths. Cast iron rainwater goods were introduced in the late 18th century as an alternative to lead. At the Blue Bell Inn, Crookham, there is a cast iron hopper head discharging into a standard, circular section downpipe (see page 138). This one is not very elaborate but it still adds to the appearance of the head of the downpipe.

A stately home or a manor house would often have very intricate designs, sometimes with the owner's monogram, such as the magnificent hopper head at Pallinsburn House shown on page 121.

Other ironwork can be seen in the villages in the form of hinges, door-knobs and knockers, door latches, door letter openings and escutcheon plates (around keyholes). This door from a former shop in Crookham has two scrolled strap hinges that may be of cast iron as they appear to be identical. Wrought iron, forged by hand, will not result in completely identical products although they may well be very close in appearance. Wrought iron has a hand-finished look about it, giving it (generally) an unmistakeable appearance. Examples of decorative hinges on doors may be seen on pages 76 and 77, including the one on the left, and also showing hinges on a church door and a village hall door. Farm doors on page 77 and 79 have simple, but strong, strap hinges. The hinges on this old workshop door (shown below) at the old dairy in Crookham are definitely rustic and made of hand-forged, wrought iron and could date from anytime within the 18th or 19th centuries. They were probably forged at the Blacksmith's Shop on the other side of the street where TillVAS carried out test-pits excavations in 2016.

The very rural communities of the four villages tend to have more workmanlike door and window furniture, so there are no showy doorknobs, letter openings or other fittings. Many of the notable buildings have quite unpretentious door furniture but there are two impressive bronze door knockers on the main north door of Pallinsburn House (see above). They bear the Mitchell arms and would have been installed during Major Charles Mitchell's alterations to the house during the early 20th century.

Branxton, Crookham and Ford possess examples of late 19th century cast iron water pillars of a style that can still be seen throughout Britain wherever they have, thankfully, been preserved. If a device was connected to a running water supply, it was not a pump and there is no pump handle. These pillars are of a standard 'lion's head' pattern with a control knob at the side and a plant finial on top like the one at Branxton (see left); the lion's head could act as the spout but these examples also have outlets above the lions' heads which would originally have held taps. In Ford, the pillar stands in front of what is shown on the 1897 OS map as a village fountain. This was on the line of a gravity-fed fresh water supply to Ford Castle including the Waterford fountain and the walled garden. There must have been a mass production of pillars because there are two identical Grade II listed pillars in the village of Acomb, near Hexham in Northumberland. These two, together with the nearby trough, were made by the Glenfield Company of Kilmarnock. The three items have been dated to before 1899 when the firm's name changed to Glenfield and Kennedy.[26] The pillar in Crookham (see right) retains the iron cup on a chain; the pillars retain their stands for holding buckets.

The cast iron water pillar in front of what was previously a fountain at Ford.

There is no surviving pillar in Etal and local tradition states that the villagers used to draw water from St. Mary's Well next to the site of the 14th century Chantry Chapel above the River Till. But tucked into a corner of a hedge and a cottage near the gatehouse at Etal Castle is this disused water spout and drain set into what were, perhaps, stones from the castle.

More mundane examples of metalwork can be seen, but ones that are performing a vital function. The photo shows one of several steel plates on the side of the old dairy in Crookham. These are connected by threaded steel rods passing through the building to corresponding plates on the opposite outside wall. They have been installed in response to the outward 'bowing' of the walls and settlement of the building. The rods will be hidden from view within the building by passing them below or through the flooring. It is interesting that, rather than minimising the visual aspect, the plates have been painted red to match the windows, or perhaps it was in order to finish the tin!

Branxton and Crookham were fortunate in retaining examples of disused cast iron, red telephone boxes in their original positions. These are rapidly becoming part of village history and, if possible, should be retained for some other useful purpose. In Branxton, the former telephone box (left) has been converted into a miniature visitors' centre and is being looked after and well-maintained by the village community. The box in Crookham (right) was situated next to the former post office and village shop but has since been taken away. The boxes appear to be the K6 type designed by Sir Giles Gilbert Scott to commemorate the Silver Jubilee of King George V in 1935. Etal has a more modern, but disused, telephone box, an aluminium and glass KX100, a type first introduced in 1985.

The former post office at Crookham, still retains a carved, one-piece, sandstone posting slot below the left-hand, ground floor window. It is in the wall of the front extension that was built in 1910. Note the attractive veins in the sandstone.

Letter boxes in current use in the villages are of wall and lamp box design rather than pillar boxes. This 19th century wall box at Ford has VR above the letter slot which, because of its width, was probably modified in the 1950s. Lamp boxes were not only attached to lamp posts but could have their own post or be attached to telegraph posts.[27]

Unlike wall boxes which had been in use from about 1857, lamp boxes were introduced in about 1897 and were intended for locations where there was a lower volume of mail. This lamp box at Branxton (left) has its own supporting post. It is interesting, not because of its age, but because it is of a kind used in Scotland. This reflects its location, being served by Royal Mail premises and personnel in Coldstream, Scottish Borders. There is no EIIR cipher, reflecting the fact that when the first Elizabethan post boxes were unveiled in Scotland, a number were vandalised and even blown up, challenging the Queen's title of Elizabeth II instead of Elizabeth I of Scotland. Although a legal challenge failed in 1953, the GPO (at that time) decided that all post boxes in Scotland should have the image of the Scottish crown with no EIIR. Therefore, although situated in England, all post boxes in Branxton, Crookham, Etal and Ford that were installed after 1953 are Scottish boxes because they are serviced from Scotland.

The history of buildings does not always include attractive examples and the redundant telephone exchange at Crookham is certainly not a building of beauty. Nevertheless, it is part of the story of the village and, even for this utilitarian building, the GPO's (at that time) architect has tried to relieve the monotonous effect by incorporating decorative, staggered, red tiles that act as kneelers below the gable ends of the roof.

The disused telephone exchange at Crookham.

However, this functional and ordinary building does allow us to mention the use of 'rendering' (harling in Scotland) as an external surface coating to give added protection against the elements. Rendering dates back to at least Roman times when mixtures of volcanic ash, sand and lime were applied to mud, brick or block walls. It can give added protection against the elements provided that no faults develop, such as cracks in the surface which enable moisture to be trapped behind the render. Architects have always specified rendering, not only as a means to improve protection against the weather and increase acoustic and thermal properties but also to improve the appearance of a building that has different or inferior surface coatings and colours.

Traditionally, lime render was used with the lime being mixed with sand and water and applied in one or two coats to provide a breathable coating. The later use of cheaper, cement render (Portland cement, lime and water), as used on the walls of the telephone exchange, produced a much harder waterproof coating, but one which was subject to the same disadvantages as discussed earlier in relation to cement mortar.

Various surface treatments may be applied to the render such as a simple, coloured limewash. Alternatively, a textured finish may be created when small pebbles are mixed in with the render to create 'roughcast'. If the small pebbles are thrown on to the surface of the wet top-coat, this is known as pebble-dash. If small, angular, sharp flints or 'marble' chips are thrown on to the surface, this is known as 'spar-dash'. The old telephone exchange appears to have a rather worn looking spar-dash finish.

Many period features to be seen in Branxton and Crookham are hidden away and can often only be seen by entering land with the permission of the owner. An example of this is the high wall separating the rear gardens of the former post office in Crookham and the house to the west. The wall is said to have been built as an imposing boundary wall between the Ford Estate and the Pallinsburn Estate. Its height of some seven feet or so does suggest something more than a garden boundary wall and many of the stones are impressive in their size. Two stones, in particular, to the left of the hanging basket bracket and immediately below the coping, are regular, squared blocks and look as though they have been reused or were intended to be used in the construction of what became the former Post Office but were surplus to construction requirements. The massive coping stones are certainly worthy of an estate boundary.

Old boundary wall between the Ford and Pallinsburn Estates. View from the west side.

We like to go about with our heads in the air, not from any misplaced sense of our own importance, but in order to see things that would be missed at a higher level. For example, bell cotes (or bellcotes) and belfrys can be seen in all four villages. Whereas a belfry is a tower

Aspects of Buildings and Monuments: Branxton, Crookham, Etal, Ford

enclosing one or more bells, housed in a small room with a roof, a bell cote is a small shelter for bells, often with a gable or shed roof and much more open to the elements. St. Paul's Church, Branxton (see left & page 94) has a belfry with ashlar quoins and rybats, a stone pyramid roof and paired, round-arched openings with a central column with a cushion capital above a string course.

The structure probably dates from the 1849 refurbishment of the church. The United Reformed Church at Crookham (previously the English Presbyterian Church) has a bell cote of cast stone with a geometric design (see right) that was built in 1932. The Chapel of the Blessed Virgin Mary at Etal also has a bell cote (see left) dating from 1858 with an exotic description in its listing, 'a steeply-gabled bell cote between nave and chancel has a pair of cusped ogee bell openings and, above, an oval opening with two mouchettes and a quatrefoil'.[28]

St Michael and All Angels Church, Ford, dates from the 13th century and was restored and altered in the 19th century. It has what looks like a belfry (see left) but the openings are exposed to the elements and there is no internal access to the bells from the tower. However, inside the church, there are faint signs of (perhaps) a spiral stair which might once have given access to the bells. Pevsner describes it as a bell cote being 'archaeologically as interesting as it is architecturally successful…a sturdy, masculine structure… It stands on a broad heavy central buttress up the W front like a chimney breast'.[29] There are two bells behind lancet openings within the first stage of the bell cote but no bell behind the single lancet above. Perhaps there was a third bell at one time. The bell cotes at Etal and Ford both have prominent wind vanes.

Coming back down to earth, Rev. Hastings Neville, Rector of Ford, mentions in 1909, 'A great many of our people still keep a pig, generally those who are the most thrifty and industrious'.[30] He goes on to describe customs and superstitions connected with pig keeping but the inference is that, by the beginning of the 20th century, individual, domestic rearing close to cottages in the villages, was on the wane. Nevertheless, there will be residents in this area who remember pigs being kept by cottagers much later into the 20th century. Many of the cottagers would have kept a pig which would not have been reared there but bought as a piglet and then fattened up on leftovers, beech-nuts and acorns, at no great cost. Depending upon custom, the slaughtered pig would be shared with others in the village, such as family and friends or with those who had helped with looking after it, or people who had helped by gathering nuts and acorns. Rev. Hastings Neville tells us that 'The killing of the pig is an important event...There is a tea party of neighbours, and the best cake is baked...The pig is never killed during a waning moon. The moon must be either increasing or full'.[31] There are still old pig stys in the villages that are now used for other purposes.

A former pig sty in Crookham with the open run in the foreground and the animal's quarters behind.

This pig sty has been solidly built with the pig being formerly housed in a lean-to extension at the end of a barn (a common method) which had a stone-built run next to it. Now it provides ideal inside and outside storage for garden equipment. Note the quality of the stonework with a large lintel above the doorway and with the walls of the run being built, not in random rubble, but in large, squared blocks built to courses and surmounted by an impressive coping. The original lime mortar is still in place. This must have been a sty fit for a prize pig, which is what they would have been anyway to the cottager. The quality of the stonework on the pig sty is a reminder of the skill of the masons in implementing the often elaborate designs of so many features to be seen in the four villages that were built during the 19th century and earlier.

It is always worth looking around in order to spot things which are often not noticed or are dismissed as being uninteresting, mundane features. For example, gate piers perform a useful function but they can also be decorative objects that enhance an entrance in such a way as to define the status of a property. Their design may be such that, not only is a mansion house listed, but the gate piers in their own right. We have already shown some examples of high status gate piers such as the listed piers

151

next to the ornate gates south of Etal Manor (page 14) and next to the ornate gates at St. Michael's Church at Ford (page 136). The pier (shown on page 151) on the A697 road at the start of Lady Waterford's Flodden Strip leading to Flodden Hill, is not as grand but it still makes a statement.

Wall piers rather than gate piers are purely architectural and decorative features at the end of a wall or within the length of a wall. Even non-listed gate piers and wall piers can be elaborate and interesting and the wall pier (left) is on the B6354 road near the junction with the A697 road. It must have been built by the same estate mason (at that time, Ford Estate) as the gate pier described on page 151 as they have similar coping designs as well as similar chamfered edges to the arrises. The bodies of the piers in both cases are constructed of sandstone ashlar blocks and the whole feel of the piers is one of high status, befitting the estate on which both were sited, some time during the 19th century.

We could not leave out the stone mounting block and the stone steps into the churchyard at St. Michael's Church, Ford. The rusticated gate pier, which we have mentioned before, together with the gates, steps and mounting block, are listed as Grade II and probably date from the 18th century. Traditionally, the mounting block has steps on only one side.

The steps into the churchyard would have allowed pedestrian access without opening the large gates and, at the same time, would have deterred unwanted animals.

The 5-step mounting block and 4-step churchyard steps, Ford.

Finally, the impressive Grade II listed gate piers and screen wall at the West Lodge of Ford Castle demonstrate the confidence of 19th century architecture.[32] The adjoining lodge has Lady Waterford's monogram on the gable and a date of 1866 so it is probable that the gate piers and screen were built at the same time. The listing details state that the Scottish architect, David Bryce, was responsible for their design.[33]

153

The castellated octagonal piers are flanked by arcades of twenty pointed arches. The rearing horses were added by the 1st Baron Joicey after his acquisition of the Ford estate in 1907. Only the hinges remain from where once hung ornamental wrought iron gates.

Gate Piers and part of the screen wall at West Lodge, Ford Castle.

In this chapter we have looked at a diverse range of 'bits and pieces'; our choice has been very subjective and has been rather a 'pick and mix' selection. Some features may appear to be ordinary at first glance but turn out to be less so on investigation. By stopping, looking around (and often upwards) we can often discover all sorts of things.

We believe this to be particularly so with the features in the next chapter.

7
Monuments and Memorials

It may not appear obvious to include monuments in a work that deals with buildings and building features. However the following are very much part of the built environment and often so ubiquitous that they escape the detailed notice that is their due. Some memorials, particularly war memorials, have a two-fold function. They speak loudly to us all. Such memorials keep in remembrance somebody who has made the ultimate sacrifice of their life but additionally they offer a comfort to those who grieve, who then know that the name of the lost will be carried forward into the future. Other memorials mark an occasion or national event or an important battle site. Public-spirited deeds made by some personage of note can also be counted in this category.

Ancient monuments, of which one is described below, are in a different category. They are there in the landscape as they have been since prehistoric times. We note their presence without knowing why they are there. Their survival in our modern prosaic landscape is subject to endless speculation and conjecture. Many words have been written, many theories aired, usually based on the necessarily limited knowledge (in this context) of the writer or speaker. But no-one can ever know what was in the minds of the people who added intriguing features to what was likely to be the sacred ritual landscape of their time. Over time humankind has had a compulsion to put into tangible form, various totems, secular or sacred, which honour their beliefs or comfort their superstitions, but which, unlike buildings, often have no useful function that we can discern. However, there is some evidence that the ritual landscape of the cairns and stone circles which drove the lives of the people of the Neolithic had changed by the late Bronze Age. The emphasis began to be on memorials which highlighted the heroic world and the commemoration of individuals and their deeds.[34]

A further category of monuments that do have a useful function is dealt with below and, later on, in Mileposts and Milemarkers.

Memorials, Wells and Ancient Stones

Branxton Memorial Drinking Fountain: The drinking fountain in the centre of Branxton was erected in 1910 in memory of Watson Askew Robertson, 1834-1906. The *Northumberland* edition of *The Buildings of England* Pevsner series, however, lists it as 'In memory of *William* [our italics] Askew Robertson', which is incorrect. It is Grade II listed.

The Watson Askew Robertson Memorial Drinking Fountain also provides a welcome meeting place.

The memorial is built of pink sandstone, in the Classical style with an elaborate cornice above and carved rectangular panels of bunches of fruit on either side set into plain pilasters.[35] The Memorial is flanked on both sides by a seat set into a curving sandstone wall. A stone basin with a grid-iron bucket stand, sits below under an attractive, possibly bronze, spout which is now defunct and an iron drainage grating sits at the front. The Memorial has suffered from the passage of time but is generally in a good condition in spite of surface accretions and the odd knock or two.

Mrs Robertson engaged a well-known and prolific Northumbrian architect, George Reavell, junior, 1865-1947, to design the Memorial. He numbered among his other commissions work on Bamburgh and Warkworth Castles and Coldstream West United Free Church (now Coldstream Community Centre). He became a Fellow of the Royal Institute of British Architects and was appointed OBE; he died in 1947.

Watson Askew Robertson of Pallinsburn died in November 1906 and his widow, the Hon. Sarah Askew Robertson, unveiled the Memorial Fountain to her deceased husband in July 1910. She was the heiress of Ladykirk when she married Watson Askew of Pallinsburn, and he added her surname, Robertson, to his. They had eight children and she died in 1929.

Flodden Memorial: This plain but impressive polished cross of Aberdeen granite stands on the eminence known as Piper's Hill or Stock Law at the foot of Branxton Hill. It sits on a base of rough granite in a rectangular gravelled enclosure. Enfolded by the land on which the opposing Scottish and English armies faced each other during the Battle of Flodden on 9th

September 1513, its isolated and commanding position is a fitting memorial to those who fell on that day.

The Flodden Memorial looking towards Branxton Hill Farm on the horizon.

The name Piper's Hill by which the memorial site has become known derives perhaps from 'Pipard's Hill' which John Stow mentioned in his *Chronicles* published in 1565, and which he described as a small hill overlooking the village of Branxton.[36] By 1858, the vicar of Branxton, the Rev. Robert Jones, described it as 'the Piper's Hill of the Royal Chronicle' and this name, repeated throughout the nineteenth century, came into general usage. The memorial was commissioned by the Berwickshire Naturalists Club as a result of a fundraising campaign and erected in 1910. An inscribed bronze plaque set into the base reads simply 'Flodden 1513, To the Brave of Both Nations, Erected 1910'. It is Grade II listed.

Marmion's Well (Sybil's Well): The spring which empties into this well has been there for a long time but came into prominence when Sir Walter Scott, in his poem *Marmion: A Tale of Flodden Field*, has the mortally wounded false knight of that name, who fought on the English side in the battle, quenching his thirst from the spring. Scott describes how '… water clear as diamond-spark, in a stone basin fell'.[37]

Marmion's Well has a mysterious feel to it, perhaps because of its dark setting amidst woodland.

The well itself was reconstructed in the late nineteenth century by Louisa, Marchioness of Waterford. Traditionally it has been said to be 'the soldiers' well'. Set into the bedrock of Flodden Ridge, the well looks north over the scattered farms and settlements towards the Scottish border. An ashlar slab forming a shallow canopy sits above the round carved hole which catches the flow of the water, set in an angular basin. The spout above the basin is evidently missing although the hole for it is quite obvious. Inscribed above the basin is a cross and in 'olde' English letters are the words,

> Drink weary pilgrim drink and stay ['pray' originally in *Marmion*]
> For the kind soul of Sybil Grey...[38]

A stone slab forming a seat sits at the right-hand side. Whether Sybil Grey was a real person or a creation of Scott's imagination is not known and although there was a well-known local family of Greys who lived at Milfield Hill House the only known record of a Sybil Grey in the family tree shows that she died in 1872. Therefore she cannot be the one referred to by Scott.[39]

Often confused with the above is the following well which was only recently listed Grade II in 1988.

<u>Branxton Well (sometimes also called Marmion's Well or Sybil Grey's Well)</u>: The well below Branxton Church is set into the bank on a bend at the south side of a narrow road. This road leads from Branxton village west, north and west to Branxton Buildings and then west and north to the A697 Coldstream to Wooler road.

Monuments and Memorials

Branxton Well in summer cloaked in common nettle and other weeds.

Branxton Well in winter, having been cleared to reveal the two troughs.

This well has not always been easy to find and, when first seen in summer months, was surrounded by nettles and other rank plants with the spring barely visible before it fell into a stone trough. By winter 2015-2016 the site had been completely cleared and the well was revealed in all its attractiveness. At this point the bank at the roadside is strengthened by a random rubble wall into which the well is set, backed by a simple stone slab, partially moss-covered. A large stone cross is carved on the slab; at each corner of the slab and at the corners of the arch that encloses the spring, are carved Celtic knots. The water emerges in a trickle from a spout, probably of bronze, within the arch and falls into a small rectangular trough. To the left is a larger rectangular 'overflow' trough. Inscribed on the face of the slab in worn Gothic lettering is the same quote from *Marmion*, this time with the correct word 'pray' instead of 'stay'. Permission was sought in 1912 to build a fountain at the well and an appeal was launched to pay for it. The present well probably dates from about 1935 and was constructed by Pattersons of Branxton.

King's Stone: This is an example of a built feature that keeps in remembrance people and a time about which we know little. It provides a link with the distant past and is vocal in its silence. Prominent in isolation, it stands on slightly higher ground at the outer edge of a field on land farmed at Crookham Westfield. Known as a 'menhir', from the words *men* and *hir* in Breton meaning *stone* and *long*, it is now bounded by a hedge on its northern side but when it was first placed here, it must have commanded an extensive all-round view. The stone is about 2.5 metres high and has been dated to between the late Neolithic Age and the early Bronze Age (approx. 3000BC-2000BC).[40] However, this is conjecture as the stone itself gives no clues to its past other than it is clearly ancient. It is a rough column of possibly Carham limestone which may have been put in its position by human hand or carried to the spot by glaciation. It is weather-worn and craggy with numerous cracks and interstices over its surface. This weathering is known as 'rillenkarren'.[41]

The King's Stone, looking towards Branxton Hill in the distance.

Whether the King's Stone was ever part of a stone circle or linked to other standing stones in the area is impossible to know. It has been well known over historic centuries as an important gathering point for, for example, armies going north or south, and in its prehistoric origin may have been a tribal gathering place or place of ceremony. It is known as the King's Stone coming from the supposition that it marks the spot where James IV was killed during the Battle of Flodden, a misapprehension given credence probably by Sir Walter Scott. But that is what gives it its particular present-day significance apart from its intrinsic importance as a prehistoric column. It is now a Scheduled Monument.

Gate Piers: There are two other stones in a field at a bend of the River Till at Crookham (see photo below). Previously used as gate piers, as evidenced by vestiges of ironwork, they stand above the river opposite Letham Hill Haugh on the footpath which leads to the site of the old cable ferry crossing opposite Etal Castle. These heavily weathered and lichened sandstone monoliths are clearly of some age and may have been part of the prehistoric ceremonial landscape of the area. Alternatively, it can be speculated that they may have been stones taken from the ruins of the medieval bridge below Etal Castle and transported across the flat field in the background.

We shall now consider some other features of the landscape which have a much more practical and, indeed, obvious, use.

Mileposts and Milemarkers

From the earliest times, humankind has always needed some means of recording distance. Perhaps the first distance measurements related simply to the time it took to travel between two set points such as settlements. Ancient peoples, particularly in the Mediterranean, travelled most often by sea, hugging the coastlines, as movement by land was fraught with danger from various predators both animal and human. Traders moved in large groups or caravans and used long established and time-honoured routes where possible through valleys and passes. Unlike our own times, travel was unlikely to have been undertaken for pleasure. It was during the Persian Empire that a policed road system was first set up with staging posts, probably initially for the purposes of conquest. This was further developed by the Greeks who, having begun in archaic times to use and name parts of the human body to denote units of measure, began to travel more widely in later times for festivals, games, and education (not to mention war and exploration) across the wider Greek world and beyond.

The values for the start and finish lines in stadia derived from the standard measurement of the human foot. The Greeks also used the word 'stathmos', from which comes our word 'station', for measured stages over a length of distance. How this was calculated differed from city to city, with that of the city of Athens becoming predominant. The Romans improved on this by the introduction of their own system of milemarkers, commonly known as milestones or mileposts, set up to measure distances, with the first milestones erected on the Appian Way outside Rome. The word 'mile' comes from the Latin words 'milia passuum' meaning 'one thousand paces'. The Roman markers were made of stone but since Roman times most countries with a developed road system have used some sort of distance marker made of other materials including concrete, iron and wood and with measurements in miles, metres or kilometres. In the UK, distances from London are measured in miles from a reference point marked by a plaque near the Eleanor Cross close to Charing Cross Station.

Milepost near the Blue Bell Inn (below): Almost opposite the Blue Bell, on the A697 Coldstream to Wooler, stands a cast iron milestone, shaped like a three-dimensional triangle with a steeply canted top and now rust and cream coloured. It dates from the early nineteenth century. On one side is inscribed MOR (Morpeth) and on the other COR (Cornhill) with the respective mileages of each—40 and 4. On the top are the initials L and E (London and Edinburgh) with the respective mileages of 327 and 51. It is Grade II listed. As with the following, it is fairly unobtrusive especially during summer months when it is lost among the long grasses of the verge.

Monuments and Memorials

Milepost, circa ¼ mile south of Pallinsburn (below, left): Dating from the early 19th century, this is in the same triangular pattern as above with a similar steeply canted top and made of now weathered cast iron. On the left-hand face is a large hole but the letters MOR are still plainly visible. On the right hand is COR with the respective mileages 41 and 3. On the canted top are the letters L and E (London and Edinburgh) with mileages 328 and 50. Grade II listed.

Milepost, circa 200 yards west of Mount Pleasant (below, right): The same triangular pattern as above with MOR on the left-hand side and COR on the right hand with the letters L and E on the top. Respective mileages 38 and 5 and 326 and 52. Grade II listed.

Milepost circa ¼ mile south east of Barelees (left): This milepost is described in the *British Listed Schedules* as being partly buried. However, two visits by both of us failed to find any trace of it in its original position shown on the Ordnance Survey map. A further search

167

revealed that it stands, now out of its original context, prominently whitewashed, with black lettering, on the opposite side of the road at the entrance to Barelees Farm. It follows the same pattern as the milestones described above, with MOR on the left side and COR on the right and L and E on the top. Respective mileages were 42 and 2 and 329 and 49.

We could not find another recorded milepost near Oakhall, Crookham.

Milemarker at the entrance to Etal Village (below, left): A cast iron marker comprising two linked ovals, with Berwick 10 miles, on the left-hand oval and Wooler 10 miles, on the right-hand.

Milemarker at Ford Bridge (below, right): A similar cast iron marker to the above, slightly to the right of the Lodge to Ford Castle.

War Memorials

These represent poignant remembrances of those who were killed serving their country in times of war and also those who served and survived. They fulfil two purposes—to honour and remember those who are lost and to offer pride and comfort into the future to those who grieve.

St. Paul's Church, Branxton: A Branxton School commemorative board for 'old' scholars who fought in the First World War hangs to the left as one enters the porch. The eight names of those killed head the list, then below are the forty-five names of those who served and survived. There is another board recording the names of the same 'old' scholars in Branxton Concrete Menagerie.

Commemorative Board for Branxton School Old Scholars.

The First World War Memorial in Branxton Church sits under two long narrow vertical stained-glass windows. The dedication on the stone memorial reads (with the letter 'U' inscribed as 'V')

THE WINDOWS ABOVE HAVE BEEN PLACED
IN THIS CHVRCH IN HONOVR OF THOSE
WHO FELL IN THE GREAT WAR OF 1914-1919

followed by a listing of nine names. The name of one of the fallen, James Patterson, also appears on the memorial now in Crookham Village Hall. The other War Memorial in the church is a rectangular brass plaque set below the memorial above which commemorates a member of the Royal Air Force who was killed in the Second World War, and a dedication to the owner of Pallinsburn House, dated 1964. See images on page 171.

First World War Memorial Windows, St. Paul's Church, Branxton.

First and Second World War Memorial Plaques, St. Paul's Church, Branxton.

<u>Crookham Village Hall</u>: Three plaques, each set horizontally above each other, and in polished wooden surrounds, were originally in Crookham School and are now hung above the door leading out of the main hall. The first rectangular plaque is centred above the second plaque as a heading to the plaques below. It reads

CROOKHAM COUNCIL SCHOOL

The second plaque is inscribed:

IN MEMORY OF THE OLD BOYS OF THIS
SCHOOL WHO FELL AND WHO SERVED
IN THE EUROPEAN WAR 1914-1918

Then follows the third much larger rectangular plaque, listing the names of those commemorated, with a horizontal line dividing the names of the six warriors who fell, from those of the thirty-three who survived.

171

Aspects of Buildings and Monuments: Branxton, Crookham, Etal, Ford

CROOKHAM COUNCIL SCHOOL		
IN MEMORY OF THE OLD BOYS OF THIS SCHOOL WHO FELL AND WHO SERVED IN THE EUROPEAN WAR 1914-1918		
JOHN ARCHBOLD	PTE	K.O.Y.L.I.
WM. AYNSLEY	GNR	R.G.A.
JAS. A. BROWN	L. CPL	A.S.S.H.
A. KIRKUP	PTE.	CANADIANS
JAS. PORTEOUS	PTE.	N.F.
W. WILKINSON	PTE.	K.O.Y.L.I.
ALEX. AYNSLEY	SGT.	A.O.C.
T. AUCHTERLONIE	PTE.	A.& S.H.
ALB. BROWN	PTE.	N.F.
AND. BROWN	CPL.	N.F.
D. BROWN	PTE.	N.F.
J. BROWN	PTE.	N.F.
L. BROWN	PTE.	R.D.G.
R. BROWN	PTE.	N.F.
A. CURLE	PTE.	R.F.
J. CURLE	PTE.	R.A.V.C.
R. CURLE	SGT.	K.R.R.
G. CONQUER	PTE.	R.A.S.C.
J. CONQUER	PTE.	R.A.F.
E. DODDS	PTE.	CANADIANS
J. B. HOGARTH	CAPT.	R.A.M.C.
T. HUME	CPL.	R.A.S.C.
R. V. JOHNSTONE	PTE.	K.O.S.B.
H. KIRKUP	PTE.	D.L.I.
J. LOWRIE	PTE.	N.F.
R. MOFFAT	PTE.	S.G.
J. MCARTHUR	2ND LIEUT.	N.F.
A. MCDOUGAL	PTE.	N.F.
J. McLEAN	PTE.	AUSTRALIANS
JAS. PATTERSON	PTE.	N.F.
JNO. PATTERSON	PTE.	R.G.A.
J. PIERCY	PTE.	N.F.
A. PRINGLE	PTE.	M.G.C.
A. ROBSON	PTE.	R.S.
J. ROMANES	PTE.	S.H.
T. ROMANES	PTE.	S.G.
G. W. SCOTT	PTE.	R.E.
T. STEWART	SGT.	R.F.A.
T. WALKER	PTE.	R.S.

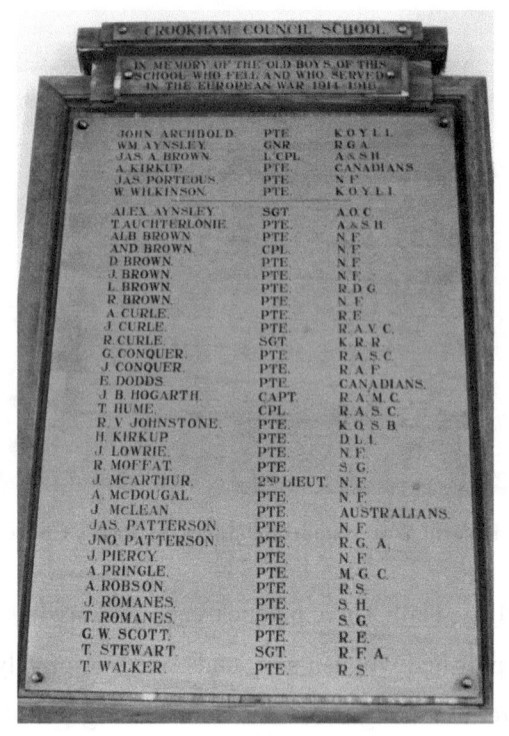

Memorial plaques in Crookham Village Hall.

Crookham United Reformed Church (former English Presbyterian Church): Often as families move away from the district, knowledge of those listed on memorials can be lost. There are two War Memorials inside the church, the first being a plaque commemorating Church members from 1914-1918. The First World War memorial includes two sets of brothers, a fact that conveys an additional poignancy—the Logan and the Hunter brothers, two sons lost at a stroke to each of their families. Taking as an example, the names of the Hunter brothers brings them into the light and illustrates their identity by noting one simple fact that they were the sons of the schoolmaster at Milfield School who retired in 1919. As the plaque eloquently says beneath the listed names, they were

"FAITHFUL UNTO DEATH"

The Second World War memorial comes in the very tangible form of the organ at the back of the church which was installed in 1948; the accompanying plaque lists five names over the inscription,

THEY DIED THAT WE MIGHT LIVE.

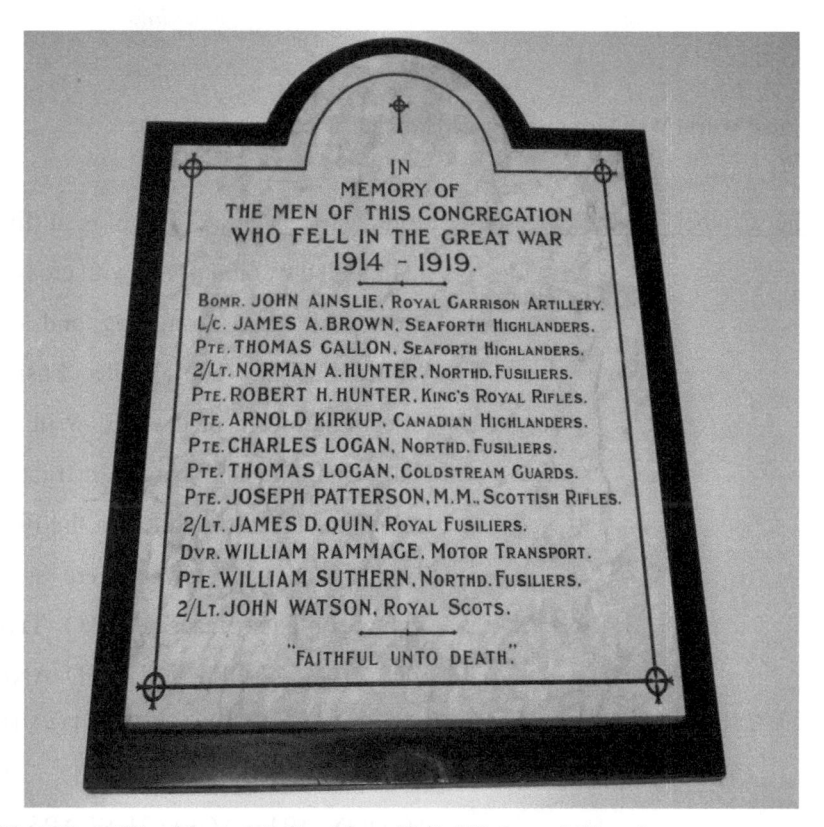

IN
MEMORY OF
THE MEN OF THIS CONGREGATION
WHO FELL IN THE GREAT WAR
1914 - 1919.

BOMR. JOHN AINSLIE, ROYAL GARRISON ARTILLERY.
L/C. JAMES A. BROWN, SEAFORTH HIGHLANDERS.
PTE. THOMAS GALLON, SEAFORTH HIGHLANDERS.
2/LT. NORMAN A. HUNTER, NORTHD. FUSILIERS.
PTE. ROBERT H. HUNTER, KING'S ROYAL RIFLES.
PTE. ARNOLD KIRKUP, CANADIAN HIGHLANDERS.
PTE. CHARLES LOGAN, NORTHD. FUSILIERS.
PTE. THOMAS LOGAN, COLDSTREAM GUARDS.
PTE. JOSEPH PATTERSON, M.M., SCOTTISH RIFLES.
2/LT. JAMES D. QUIN, ROYAL FUSILIERS.
DVR. WILLIAM RAMMAGE, MOTOR TRANSPORT.
PTE. WILLIAM SUTHERN, NORTHD. FUSILIERS.
2/LT. JOHN WATSON, ROYAL SCOTS.

"FAITHFUL UNTO DEATH."

First World War Memorial, Crookham United Reformed Church.

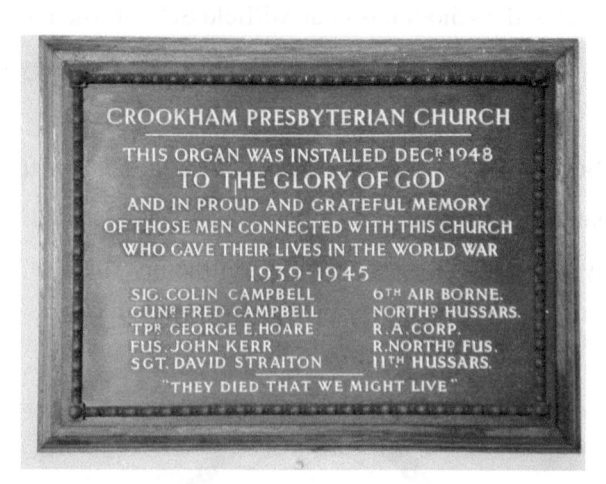

Second World War Memorial, Crookham United Reformed Church.

The Chapel of the Blessed Virgin Mary at Etal: There is a fine pedimented war memorial with crossed images of the Union Flag and the White Ensign. The White Ensign reflects the death of the Rev. William Hall, Chaplain and Naval Instructor. Below are listed the fallen in the First World War (see left). There is a separate plaque inscribed TO THE GREATER GLORY OF GOD AND IN LOVING MEMORY OF DAVID HUGH JOICEY, KILLED IN ACTION, 1943, AGED 21 YEARS.

Church of St Michael and All Angels, Ford: In the centre of the south wall are the memorial plaques of the two world wars. The largest memorial has at its centre under a pediment, a depiction of St George killing the dragon. On either side of this is listed the nineteen names of those who gave their lives. Underneath is the wording

TO THE
GLORIOUS MEMORY
OF MEN OF THE
PARISH OF FORD
WHO MADE THE
SUPREME
SACRIFICE IN THE
GREAT WAR 1914-
1919

Immediately beneath this memorial is the stone plaque for the 1939-1945 war. The cross of St George is depicted in the top left-hand corner with the words next to it

TO THE MEMORY OF THOSE
FROM THIS PARISH WHO DIED IN THE WORLD WAR
1939-1945

The eleven names of those who died are listed below this memorial.

Dedication and Information Plaques

Branxton Village Hall: The foundation stone of the village hall is inscribed on the front elevation

THIS STONE WAS LAID
BY MARJORIE ASKEW
SEPT. 12 1910

Katherine Marjorie Askew was the wife of William Haggerstone Askew and daughter-in-law of Watson Askew Robertson (see pages 156/7).

Crookham United Reformed Church (formerly Crookham Presbyterian Church: The simple inscribed foundation stone (below) is situated in the vestibule of the church. The stone came from the old church which was demolished to enable the new church to be built on the same site in 1932/33. The congregation of 1745 must surely have felt some trepidation in the face of the Jacobite uprising of that year.

Foundation stone of the former Crookham English Presbyterian Church.

Two other plaques (below) can be seen inside the church. Rev. Forsyth's forty years of service and Mr Brown's sixty years of service as organist are memorable examples of dedication.

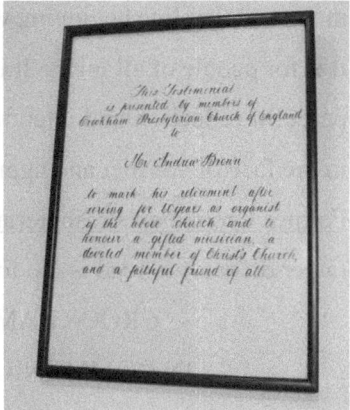

Memorial to Rev. Moses Forsyth and a Testament to Mr Andrew Brown, Crookham Church.

Low down on the front elevation of the church is

THIS CHURCH WAS OPENED

BY SIR FRANCIS D. BLAKE, BART.

C.B., D.L., J.P.

8TH JULY 1933

Also on the front elevation of the church, the Foundation Stone states:

LAID BY

SIR ARTHUR MUNRO SUTHERLAND,

BART., K.B.E., D.L., J.P.

3RD SEPT. 1932

The Peace Garden, Crookham United Reformed Church: Although not a memorial in the strictest sense of the word, it is worth briefly mentioning its existence in this narrative. The Peace Garden wraps itself around this church and is linked with the Flodden 1513 Ecomuseum and the memorial timeline beginning with the Battle of Flodden. Opened in 2017, it is for people of all faiths. It is designed to be a place of tranquillity and peaceful reflection and intended to highlight reconciliation and dialogue in the face of conflict and aggression.

Former Crookham Presbyterian School: On a worn stone which is now rather difficult to read is the following

CROOKHAM PRESBYTERIAN SCHOOL

IN COMMUNION WITH THE SYNOD OF THE

PRESBYTERIAN CHURCH IN ENGLAND

ERECTED [month?] 1856

PROV. XXII [?] [illegible thereafter]

The partly illegible lines may refer to Proverbs, Chapter 22, verse 6, 'Train up a child in the way he should go: and when he is old, he will not depart from it'. The former Presbyterian school (see right) and schoolhouse, or Master's House (to the left of the school), lie to the west of the present Crookham United Reformed Church and are now private houses.

Etal and Ford: The parishioners of the villages of Etal and Ford are blessed with two places of worship, both of which contain several features of interest. A selection of these is detailed below.

The Chapel of the Blessed Virgin Mary at Etal: This small chapel (see photo on page 43), in which services are held for the parishioners during the winter months, stands at the right, just within the drive to Etal Manor. It served to replace the ancient ruined chantry chapel on the banks of the River Till. Chantries, as the name suggests, were built to offer up chants and prayers for the souls of the departed.

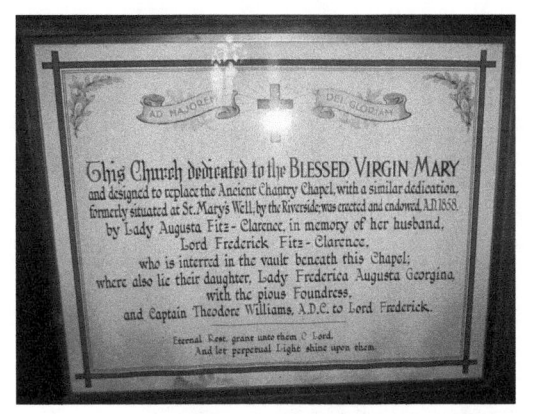

This chapel was erected in memory of Lord Frederick FitzClarence who died in India in 1854, and who lies buried within. He was originally interred in Ford Church in 1855. Lord Frederick was a son of King William IV and the actress, Dorothea Jordan. The chapel was built and endowed by his wife, Lady Augusta FitzClarence in 1858 and Lord Frederick's body was interred in the vault of the chapel in 1876. Lady Augusta died that same year and her remains also lie in the chapel alongside her husband, their only daughter, Lady Frederica, and son-in-law, Captain Theodore Williams, who was Lord Frederick's aide-de-camp. Fittingly, the armorial bearings of Lord Frederick FitzClarence are displayed within the chapel.

Etal Peace Commemoration Hall: The hall (see photo on page 101) was opened in 1926 and there is an information plaque on the front elevation.

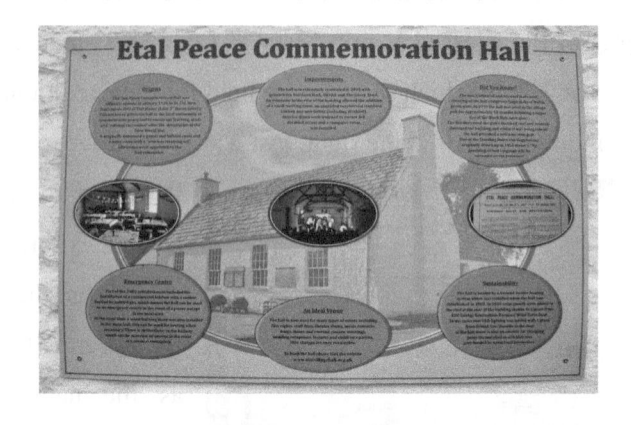

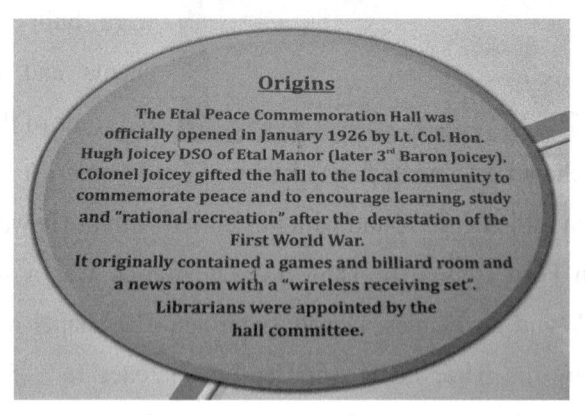

Origins
The Etal Peace Commemoration Hall was officially opened in January 1926 by Lt. Col. Hon. Hugh Joicey DSO of Etal Manor (later 3rd Baron Joicey). Colonel Joicey gifted the hall to the local community to commemorate peace and to encourage learning, study and "rational recreation" after the devastation of the First World War.
It originally contained a games and billiard room and a news room with a "wireless receiving set". Librarians were appointed by the hall committee.

One of the 'lozenges' on the plaque mentions the history of the hall. The Berwick Advertiser of 7th January 1926 described the opening ceremony which was followed by a whist drive. It was noted that the electricity was 'obtained from Colonel Joicey's generating station' described above on pages 46 and 47.

Monuments and Memorials

<u>The Church of St Michael and All Angels at Ford</u>: A complete contrast with the chapel at Etal is Ford Church in which services for the two villages are held during the summer months. As can be expected for a church with such an ancient foundation (it dates from the 13th century) there are a large number of features which span the ages, from the sombre ancient stone grave slabs set in the floor at the back of the church, through family dedications and remembrances of the clerics who served the parish, to the vibrant stained glass which lights the interior. A selection is described below.

On entering the porch, one's attention is drawn to a cast-iron plaque which emphasises the importance then held of welcoming all, of whatever degree, to take part in worship. It states

A Grant of £100 towards the

ENLARGEMENT

of this Church was made by the

Incorporated Society for Promoting

The Enlargement, Building, and Repair

ing (sic) of Churches and Chapels on the

express and acknowledged condition

that 200 Seats should be reserved

for the use of the Poorer Inhabitants

of this Parish for ever; such Seats

being distinguished by the numbers

1 to 27 both

inclusive

181

The figures of '£100', '200' and '1 to 27' and the word 'Enlargement' have clearly been inserted into the plaque at a later date. Entering through the inner door, the immediate dimness of the church is lightened by the number of stained-glass windows which commemorate the great and good of the parish, from the late eighteenth century onwards.

The George Culley Window: Together with his brother, George Culley was a prominent and innovative farmer, not just in the parish but throughout Northumberland. The eye is immediately attracted by this window which is opposite the entrance. It depicts a shepherd with a crook standing against the background of a stretch of water described as the River Jordan, in front of a line of hills. Arranged in a triangle below is the quotation from Genesis, chapter 32, verse 10

I am not worthy of the least of all
thy mercies and of all the truth, which thou hast
served unto thy
servant

At the bottom of the window is:
+ In memory of George Culley who
Departed this life 7th May 1813

Three further stained-glass windows at the rear of the church, flanking the window depicting the Archangel Michael, honour the memory of James Grey of Kimmerston who died in 1777; Delaval Knight (sic), undated; George Charles Carpenter who lived at Ford Cottage and who died in Milan in 1867. Three windows along the south wall of the church commemorate three members of the prominent Askew family who died in the nineteenth century.

The Michael Joicey Memorial Window: This beautiful stained-class window lights the east wall of the north aisle, immediately to the left of the pulpit. It commemorates the 4th Baron Joicey who died as a result of an accident on 14 June 1993. The window was commissioned by his widow, Lady Elizabeth Joicey, and was designed by the York artist, Ann Sotheran. It depicts the countryside and honours the stewardship and concern for conservation that was close to Lord Joicey's heart. Under the depiction of a rainbow which spans the whole dedication, the window is divided in two. On the right, a shepherd with his crook is shown with cradling a lamb against a background of hills and under a tree in which a red squirrel nestles eating nuts. An extract from Psalm 23 follows

        I will lift up

        Mine eyes

        Unto the hills

A fawn is shown lying down and then the words:

The Lord

Made Heaven

And Earth

The left-hand side shows a sheep dog (Border Collie), a sheep, an otter, birds and primroses and fish:

Remember before God

Michael Edward

4th Baron Joicey 28/2/25-14/6/93

Under this window is a large glass case which holds an ancient leather-bound copy of the Holy Bible and a similar leather-bound copy of the Book of Common Prayer. Both have a brass plate inside the front cover which commemorates in Latin, the 4th Earl of Glasgow, father of Lady Augusta FitzClarence. The leather bindings of each are enhanced by gilt clasps. The copy of the Holy Bible has clearly had a great deal of use over its lifetime. It is missing half its spine and is broken-backed. Also in the case is a much smaller copy of the Book of Common Prayer, bound in wood and also with gilt clasps. The date of publication is 1852, and on the right-hand flyleaf is inscribed

Lady Augusta FitzClarence

From S.I.S.P [?]

On her return from India in

January 1855.

The Peace Window: Mid-way along the north wall is a colourful and very striking stained-glass window depicting, in the centre, a figure cradling a lamb and surrounded by multi-coloured abstract glass shapes. This is the Peace Window (see right) and is dated 1972; it provides a complete contrast to the more traditional stained-glass dedications on the south wall.

Painting of the Crucifiction: This large arresting painting (see below), the gift of a former Churchwarden, hangs in the middle of the West wall near the font.

The Chancel: There are a number of interesting memorials in the chancel which highlight further the lives and servants of the church, including a second Delaval Knight (sic) memorial and one to the Reverend Thomas Knight who was the rector of Ford Parish for fifty-three years and died in 1872.

An important brass monument over the Vestry door pays tribute to Lady Louisa Waterford. This records that she is also remembered by the very tangible stone reredos on either side of the altar which was the offering to her memory of the 'many rich and poor' of the parish.

The words state

THE RIGHTEOUSNESS SHALL BE IN

EVERLASTING MEMORY—PSALM CXII

Another brass tablet placed in the church by the tenants of Ford Estate commemorates the death in 1891 of their generous benefactress, already mentioned above.

It is fitting that the last of the memorials and dedications we highlight pay tribute to four of those who also loved and cherished the surroundings in which they came to live.

<u>The Monument to Lord Frederick FitzClarence and Sir James Laing</u>: The first monument, probably erected between 1850 and 1853, is sited on private land about fifty yards to the east of Etal Manor. It is a rectangular, tapering sandstone block, five feet high, sitting on a square moulded base. This is topped by a shallow block in the form of a pyramid. It is inscribed

As a humble mark of gratitude to providence for happiness passed on these estates during a period of thirty-two years. Frederick FitzClarence had this inscription made on leaving for India.

As Lord FitzClarence died in India in 1854, these words are invested now with a certain poignancy. One wonders if his words were premonitory. Below the above in a moulded panel, and added to the monument on 11th January 1898, is a thank-offering from a later custodian of the Etal Estate, Sir James Laing. His inscription reads

As a tribute of thankfulness for the bounteous giver of all good for unnumbered mercies during his life James Laing inscribed this on his 70th Birthday.

The Waterford Fountain: This monument, a former fountain, was erected by Lady Louisa Waterford, and commemorates the death of her husband, the Marquess of Waterford, in 1859. It is an imposing pink granite column, topped by a sandstone, almost life-sized angel holding a shield emblazoned with the Waterford Arms. The column suffered storm damage in 1868 but was restored. It sits in a quatrefoil basin, with a lion's head spout at each corner.

The lettering between the spouts is worn but includes the following inscription

with joy shall ye drink out of the well of salvation.

Drink ye abundantly O Beloved

It is Grade II listed.

Memorial Stone the 4th Baron Joicey: Overlooking the River Till and alongside the footpath and cycleway at Barleymill Bank, north of Etal, is a simple stone memorial to the 4th Lord Joicey. It is near to the spot where Lord Joicey died whilst doing what he enjoyed, working in the open air on his estate. It reads

M.E.J
JUNE 14_{TH} 1993
A man greatly loved.

This selection of monuments and memorials has been chosen selectively by the writers of this account. We hope that it acts as a testament to the involvement and pride of the inhabitants of the villages and those connected with them and, that honouring past lives in this way, will continue in the future

Notes

1. Mawer, Allen, *The Place-Names of Northumberland and Durham*, Cambridge University Press, 1920, pp. 30, 58, 78, 88, 235; Mills, A D, *Dictionary of English Place-Names*, second edition, Oxford University Press, Oxford & New York, 1998, pp. 51, 103, 131; Watson, Godfrey, *Goodwife Hot and Other Places: Northumberland's Past in its Place Names*, [Oriel Press, 1970], reprinted Sandhill Press, Alnwick, 1986, pp. 37, 69, 89.

2. Mawer, p. 39; Mills, p. 71; Watson, p. 147

3. Johnson, Matthew, *English Houses 1300-1800*, Routledge, London and New York, 2014, p. 148

4. See online at https://communities.northumberland.gov.uk/Etal

5. www.ford-and-etal.co.uk/heatherslaw-mill/history

6. Hutchinson, W, *A View of Northumberland with an Excursion to The Abbey of Mailross in Scotland, Anno 1776*, Vol. II, printed by T. Saint for W. Charnley and Messrs. Vesey & Whitfield, Newcastle, 1778, pp. 337/8

7. *Historic Farmsteads. Preliminary Character Statement: North East Region*, University of Gloucestershire in association with English Heritage and the Countryside Agency, 2006, pp. 26/8

8. Roberts, Brian K & Wrathmell, Stuart, *Region and Place A Study of English Rural Settlement*, English Heritage, 2002, pp. 41/2

9. *Historic Farmsteads*, p. 28

10. See Spirit in Stone, http://www.spiritinstone.co.uk/churches/st-mary-the-virgin-church-etal&ssid=2083006

11. For more detailed information on the early 20th century electricity supply to Etal, see http://www.taylorandgreen.co.uk/the%20power%20house.html

12. Chessell, Antony, *Breamish and Till: From Source to Tweed*, TillVAS, 2014, pp. 158/9. See also a paper prepared for TillVAS by Les Turnbull, North of

England Institute of Mining Engineers, *Landsale Only: Notes on the History of Etal Colliery in the Till Valley*, April 2018

13. For 1951 Grade II* listing details see *British Listed Buildings*, Historic England Source ID: 1042162, English Heritage Legacy ID: 238088

14. For 1951 Grade II listing details see *British Listed Buildings*, Historic England Source ID: 1042191, English Heritage Legacy ID: 237969. See also Ryder, Peter, *St. Paul's Church, Branxton Northumberland An Archaeological Assessment*, November 2012. Re. porch, see pp. 1/2, 5

15. online etymology dictionary www.etymonline.com/word/window

16. *The Berwick Advertiser*, Thursday, 7th January 1926

17. www.keystothepast.info (website maintained by Durham County Council & Northumberland County Council), Ref. No. N1942 or N27599

18. 'The Primitive Methodists were a major offshoot of the principal [sic]stream of Methodism, the Wesleyan Methodists - in 19th Century Britain. In the early decades of the 19th century there was a growing body of opinion among the Wesleyans that their Connexion [sic] was moving in directions which were a distortion of, not to say a betrayal of, what John Wesley had brought to birth in the 18th century. Eventually a Methodist preacher called Hugh Bourne became the catalyst for a breakaway, to form the Primitive Methodists. Probably 'primitive' was used to clarify their self-understanding that they were the true guardians of the original, or primitive, form of Methodism.' Taken from the website of the Methodist Church www.methodist.org.uk/about-us/the-methodist-church

19. Induni, Liz, *Tin Tabernacles* www.buildingconservation.com

20. Chimney spotter, Lance Bates on the BBC 'One Show', April 2009. See www.bbc.co.uk/stoke/content/articles/2009/08/20/chimney_pot_museum_feature.shtml

21. Hutchinson, W, *A View of Northumberland with an Excursion to The Abbey of Mailross in Scotland, Anno 1776*, Vol. II, printed by T Saint for W Charnley and Messrs Vesey & Whitfield, Newcastle, 1778, pp. 337/8

Notes

22. Pevsner, Nikolaus; Richmond, Ian; Grundy, John; McCombie, Grace; Ryder, Peter; Welfare, Humphrey, *The Buildings of England Northumberland*, Second edition revised, Yale University Press, New Haven and London, 2002, p. 644

23. ibid., pp. 30-118

24. Cambridge Dictionary online, Cambridge University Press 2018. https://dictionary.cambridge.org

25. See for example www.londongardenstrust.org/features/railings3.htm

26. See www.villagepumps.org.uk/pumpsNorthumb.htm

27. www.royalmailgroup.com/sites/default/files/Royal%20Mail%20Post%20Boxes%20Heritage%20Agreement.pdf; www.wicks.org/pulp/part1.html

28. *British Listed Buildings* www.britishlistedbuildings.co.uk Grade II listing ID: 1042179. English Heritage Legacy ID: 238043

29. Pevsner, pp. 281/2.

30. Neville, Rev Hastings, *A Corner in the North: Yesterday and To-day with Border Folk,* Andrew Reid & Company Limited, Newcastle-Upon-Tyne, 1909, p. 109.

31. ibid.

32. *British Listed Buildings* Grade II listing ID: 1153904, English Heritage Legacy ID: 238034

33. David Bryce (1803-1876) was a prominent Edinburgh architect. For details of his life and career, see the Dictionary of Scottish Architects at www.scottisharchitects.org.uk/architect_full.php?id=100014

34. Armit, Ian, *Celtic Scotland: Iron Age Scotland in its European Context*, Birlinn, 2016 [1997], chap. 2, pp. 11-12

35. Pevsner, p. 200

36. Stow, John, *Annales or a Generale Chronicle of England from Brute until the present year of Christ 1580* (1580 Edition), p. 901

37. Scott, Walter, *Marmion*... Canto 6, Stanza XXX quoted in Neville, Hastings, *Under a Border Tower*, chap. XVI, p. 258-259, Newcastle, Mawson, Swan & Morgan, 2nd Ed., 1897

38. Friends of Berwick and District Museum and Archives www.berwickfriends.org.history/branxton-flodden

39. *Archaeology in Northumberland*, Vol. 20, Northumberland County Council, 2011, p. 24

40. Historic England. List Entry Number: 1002906

41. Hammond, N G L & Scullard, H H (eds.) *The Oxford Classical Dictionary*, Oxford at the Clarendon Press, 1978 [1970], Measures 1, p. 659, Travel, pp. 1089-1090

Geology Appendix

Bedrock Geology of Branxton, Crookham, Etal, Ford and Heatherslaw

Information taken from British Geological Survey Geology of Britain Viewer: http://mapapps.bgs.ac.uk/geologyofbritain/home.html?location Details of surface deposits such as siltstones, mudstones, sand, gravel and other materials which will have been deposited later by glacial action or by rivers have not been dealt with here as it is bedrock geology that is important for building purposes.

Branxton Village and surrounding area
Bedrock geology: Ballagan Formation - Sandstone, siltstone and dolomitic limestone. Sedimentary bedrock formed between 358.9 and 344.5 million years ago during the Carboniferous period. Local environment previously dominated by rivers.
Setting: ice age conditions. These sedimentary rocks are fluvial in origin. They are detrital, ranging from course to fine-grained and form beds and lenses of deposits reflecting the channels, floodplains and levees of a river.

South-east of Branxton Village
Bedrock geology: Cheviot Volcanic Formation – Andesite. Igneous Bedrock formed approximately 393 to 419 million years ago in the

Devonian Period. Local environment previously dominated by eruptions of silica-poor magma.

Setting: eruptions of silica-poor magma. These igneous rocks are volcanic (extrusive) in origin. Poor in silica, they form fluid flows of lava with feeder dykes and sills.

Crookham Village and immediately surrounding area

Bedrock geology: Ballagan Formation - Sandstone, siltstone and dolomitic limestone. Sedimentary bedrock formed between 358.9 and 344.5 million years ago during the Carboniferous period. Local environment previously dominated by rivers.

Setting: rivers. These sedimentary rocks are fluvial in origin. They are detrital, ranging from course to fine-grained and form beds and lenses of deposits reflecting the channels, floodplains and levees of a river.

South of Crookham Village

Bedrock geology: Cheviot Volcanic Formation – Andesite. Igneous Bedrock formed approximately 393 to 419 million years ago in the Devonian Period. Local environment previously dominated by eruptions of silica-poor magma.

Setting: eruptions of silica-poor magma. These igneous rocks are volcanic (extrusive) in origin. Poor in silica, they form fluid flows of lava with feeder dykes and sills.

Etal Village and north, west and south of the village

Bedrock geology: Ballagan Formation - Sandstone, siltstone and dolomitic limestone. Sedimentary bedrock formed between 358.9 and 344.5 million years ago during the Carboniferous period. Local environment previously dominated by rivers.

Setting: rivers. These sedimentary rocks are fluvial in origin. They are detrital, ranging from course to fine-grained and form beds and lenses of deposits reflecting the channels, floodplains and levees of a river.

East of Etal Village

Bedrock geology: Fell Sandstone Formation - Sandstone. Sedimentary bedrock formed between 346.7 and 337 million years ago during the Carboniferous period. Local environment previously dominated by rivers.

Setting: rivers. These sedimentary rocks are fluvial in origin. They are detrital, ranging from course to fine-grained and form beds and lenses of deposits reflecting the channels, floodplains and levees of a river.

Ford Village

Bedrock geology: Fell Sandstone Formation - Sandstone. Sedimentary bedrock formed between 346.7 and 337 million years ago during the Carboniferous period. Local environment previously dominated by rivers.

Setting: rivers. These sedimentary rocks are fluvial in origin. They are detrital, ranging from course-to fine-grained and form beds and lenses of deposits reflecting the channels, floodplains and levees of a river.

North & West of Ford Village

Bedrock geology: Fell Sandstone Formation – Sandstone. Sedimentary bedrock formed approximately 337 to 347 million years ago in the Carboniferous Period. Local environment previously dominated by rivers.

Setting: rivers. These sedimentary rocks are fluvial in origin. They are detrital, ranging from course to fine-grained and form beds and lenses of deposits reflecting the channels, floodplains and levees of a river.

South of Ford Village

Bedrock geology: Ballaghan Formation – Sandstone, siltstone and dolomite limestone. Sedimentary bedrock formed between 358.9 and 344.5 million years ago during the Carboniferous Period. Local environment previously dominated by rivers.

Setting: rivers. These sedimentary rocks are fluvial in origin. They are detrital, ranging from course to fine-grained and form beds and lenses of deposits reflecting the channels, floodplains and levees of a river.

North-east of Ford Village

Bedrock geology: Scremerston Coal Member - Sandstone, siltstone and mudstone. Sedimentary bedrock formed between 343 and 330.9 million years ago during the Carboniferous period. Local environment previously dominated by rivers.

Setting: These sedimentary rocks are fluvial, palustrine and shallow-marine in origin. They are detrital, forming deposits reflecting the channels, floodplains and deltas of a river.

Heatherslaw-West Bank

Bedrock geology: Ballagan Formation - Sandstone, siltstone and dolomitic limestone. Sedimentary bedrock formed between 358.9 and 344.5 million years ago during the Carboniferous period. Local environment previously dominated by rivers.
Setting: rivers. These sedimentary rocks are fluvial in origin. They are detrital, ranging from course to fine-grained and form beds and lenses of deposits reflecting the channels, floodplains and levees of a river.

Heatherslaw-East Bank

Bedrock geology: Fell Sandstone Formation - Sandstone. Sedimentary bedrock formed between 346.7 and 337 million years ago during the Carboniferous period. Local environment previously dominated by rivers.
Setting: rivers. These sedimentary rocks are fluvial in origin. They are detrital, ranging from course to fine-grained and form beds and lenses of deposits reflecting the channels, floodplains and levees of a river.

Glossary of Building & Other Terms

andesite	an extrusive igneous, volcanic rock
arris	the sharp edge of e.g. a quoin
Art Deco	a style of architecture prominent in the 1930s
ashlar	stones cut into rectangular blocks, polished or finely tooled, with fine mortar beds
baluster	the upright that supports a horizontal rail or coping
barge board	a timber piece fitted to the outer edge of a gable, often carved for decorative effect
basalt	a common extrusive, igneous rock
bedding plane	the level between e.g. each layer of sedimentary rock
brace	a diagonal timber between horizontal ledges of a door
broaching	the tooling of the face of dressed stone to give parallel lines
casement	a side-hinged window
cast iron	an alloy of iron, carbon and silicon, cast in a mould and hard, brittle and non-malleable
cement mortar	a modern bonding and pointing material for stonework and brickwork using cement, sand and water
cill	a stone, wood, or metal beam below a window opening
chamfer	an object with the edges of the front face angled back

Glossary of Building & Other Terms

coping	an (overhanging) section of stone on top of a wall designed to protect the wall from rainwater
corbel	a projecting piece of timber, stone or brick, supporting a cornice
cornice	a horizontal decorative moulding on top of a building feature
course	a row of stones or brick in a wall
cushion capital	a capital on top of a column used in Byzantine, Romanesque and Norman architecture shaped like a bowl with a flat top
dentilation	a series of small square blocks set into a cornice, like teeth
diapering	a decorative surface pattern using two different colour bricks and sometimes using projecting courses of bricks
dolerite	a course-grained, intrusive igneous rock
dormer having	a window wholly or partly set in a sloping roof, its own roof and side walls
dressed stone	regular masonry tooled to a fine finish
drip mould	a projection moulding that prevents rainwater from running down the face of a wall
droving	see broaching
drumlin	an elongated hill of glacial drift
eaves	the lower overhanging section of a pitched roof
escutcheon	a flat piece of metal around e.g. a keyhole

extrados	the exterior or upper curve of an arch
fascia	a board which caps the end of rafters and is used to hold the gutter
fillet	a triangular profile flashing of cement and sand or lime and sand in the angle between roof and verge or wall
finial	an ornament in stone, wood or metal at the apex of a dormer or roof
flashing	a zinc or lead apron or fillet over a joint between masonry and slates or tiles
flaunching	the sloping mortar fillet on top of a chimney stack in which the chimney pots are set
frieze	the middle section of a classical entablature (cornice, frieze, architrave)
gabbro	a coarse-grained, dark, intrusive igneous rock
gable	the end wall of a building
gable parapet	where the gable wall projects above the roof slope- usually capped with coping stones
galvanising	the coating of iron or steel with zinc to provide protection against rust
gambrel roof	a symmetrical two-sided roof with two slopes on each side
Gothic style	an architectural style developed in Western Europe between the 12th and 16th century, characterised by ribbed vaulting, flying buttresses, pointed arches, high ceilings and high, narrow windows

granite	a coarse-grained, intrusive, igneous rock
header	a brick which is laid with its greatest length at right angles to the face of the wall
headstop	a decorative boss or a right-angled termination of a drip mould
hipped roof	a roof sloping at the ends as well as the sides
hopper-head	a funnel which collects rainwater from a gutter for discharge into a downpipe
horns	timber projections below the upper window sash for strength and decoration
igneous rock	rock formed by the solidification of molten lava (extrusive or volcanic) or magma (intrusive or plutonic)
Jacobethan	a term introduced by John Betjeman in 1933 to describe the Renaissance revival style which combined elements of the Elizabethan early Renaissance style of architecture with the Jacobean late Renaissance style
intrados	the interior or lower curve of an arch
keystone	the central shaped stone in an arch or vault
kneeler	a shaped stone at the top of a wall that supports an inclined coping
lancet	a window or arch coming to a narrow point, used in Gothic architecture

lens	a body or rock or ore that is thick in the middle and
thin	at the edges like a convex lens
ledge (door)	a horizontal timber to which the boards are affixed
levee	A levee is a natural or artificial earth bank which regulates water levels. It is usually parallel to the course of a river in its floodplain.
lime mortar	a traditional bonding and pointing material for stonework and brickwork using slaked lime, sand and water
lintel	a stone or timber beam over a door or window opening
mansard	a roof that is flat on top and slopes down steeply on two or four sides
margin	a flat or tooled border worked in stone around a door
or	window opening or at the corner of a building
mouchette	a daggerlike architectural form in tracery created by a segmental and ogee curve so that it is pointed at one end and circular at the other
mullion	a vertical member between close but separate windows
muntin	the central vertical part of a frame on a panelled door
ogee	a moulding in stone, joinery or cast iron with two reverse curves like a letter S
ovolo	a rounded, convex moulding being a quarter section of a circle

Glossary of Building & Other Terms

palustrine	relating to a system of inland freshwater wetlands
pantile	a clay roof tile of S section
parapet	a protective wall e.g. at the edge of a roof or terrace
parging	a thin coat of plaster or mortar applied to rough masonry
pebbledash	an exterior wall finish of wet render on to which pebbles have been thrown
pinnings	small stone slithers used to fill up gaps and level a course
plinth	a base or platform which supports a column or other structure
plutonic rock	intrusive igneous rock formed by the solidification of molten magma
pointing	the process of filling and finishing the joints in stonework and brickwork with mortar
quatrefoil four	in architecture, a symmetrical shape consisting of overlapping circles of the same diameter
quoin	a rectangular dressed stone at the corner of a building
random rubble	rough undressed stonework of varying sizes
rebate take a	a hidden rectangular section cut out of masonry to door or window frame
rendering	the application of cement to external walls to give a smooth or textured protective coat
reveal	the visible return face of stonework or brickwork at a door or window opening

203

Roman tiles	for roofs-flat in the middle with a concave curve at one end and a convex curve at the other. The double Roman tile has an additional convex profile in the middle
Romanesque	a style of architecture containing Roman and Byzantine elements prevalent in the 11th and 12th centuries and characterised by massive walls, round arches and fairly simple ornamentation
roughcast	an exterior wall finish where gravel is mixed with the wet rendering
RSJ	rolled steel joist
rustication	an exaggerated form of masonry with recessed or V-shaped joints
rybats	dressed stones used in forming corners at door and window openings
sarking	timber boarding laid over rafters to which the roof covering is fixed
sash	a vertically sliding window pane and frame with hidden weights on rope or chain
sedimentary	a type of rock that has been deposited by water, wind or ice and solidified by pressure to form layers in a structure called bedding
shaft	in a chimney stack, the part above the plinth and below the cornice

Glossary of Building & Other Terms

slate	a fine-grained metamorphic rock that splits into smooth-surfaced layers useful for roofing
sneck	a small, square stone built into masonry, with others, to level a course
spa-dash	an exterior wall finish where 'marble' chippings are thrown onto the wet rendering
springing point	the level at which an arch starts to rise from a wall
stile	the vertical side member of a panelled door or a window
strap pointing	raised pointing, usually in cement mortar
stretcher	a brick which is laid with its greatest length on the face of the wall
string course	a decorative horizontal band of stone or brick projecting beyond or flush with the face of the wall
stugging	a picked, surface tooling on dressed stonework
terracotta	a type of earthenware where the fired clay is porous often unglazed and often reddish-brown in colour caused by the oxidation of iron. It can be used for sculpture, utilitarian vessels, roofing tiles and water and waste pipes
thatch	a roof covering of e.g. straw, reeds, rushes or heather
tooling	the working with a metal tool of the surface of masonry
torching	the application of mortar to the underside of tiles or slates

transom	a horizontal member separating window lights
trefoil	"three leaves", i.e. relating to a decorative element resembling a clover leaf
tuck pointing	insetting of narrow fillets of putty, lime or chalk into mortar joints to give an impression of fine joints
tumbled in	brickwork laid diagonally on gables to form triangles which provide a flat bed for sloping parapets
uPVC	articles made from the polymer, polyvinylchloride. uPVC is free from plasticizers used in PVC; uPVC is rigid and suitable for e.g. window frames whereas PVC is flexible and suitable for e.g. pipes
Venetian	a window composed of three openings, the central one arched, the two flanking ones with flat heads
vermiculation	a masonry finish resembling wriggling worms
vernacular	architectural style reflecting local traditions and construction materials
volcanic rock	extrusive igneous rock formed by the solidification of molten lava
voussoir	one of the wedge-shaped stone or brick blocks forming an arch
whinstone	in this book, a generic term for hard igneous building stone
wrought iron	a form of iron with a low carbon content making it tough, malleable and relatively soft

Index

Illustrations in **bold**

~

agriculture
  enclosures, 34, 131
  improvement, 33-5, 131
aluminium, 73
andesite *see* geology
arches, 79-81, **75, 79**, 80, **80**, 81, **81**
  85, **85**, 87, **87**, 92
  brick, 92, **93**
  depressed, 80
  extrados, 94
  flat or 'Jack', **93**, 94
  intrados, 94
  keystones, 80, **80**, 87, **93**, 94
  segmental, 80
  voussoirs, 81, **81**, 87, **93**, 94
Arts and Crafts, 44, **45**
Art Deco, 53
ashlar, 6, 28, 48, **49**, 50, 51, **51**, 53,
  56, 76, **76**
Askew, Marjorie, 176, **176**

~

Ballagan *see* geology
Barelees Farm, 80, **80**
barge boards *see* roofs
bedding planes, 48, **49**
basalt *see* geology
bay windows *see* windows
bell cotes, belfries, 129, **129**, 147-9,
  148, 149
Berwickshire Nat. Club, 158-9
Birdoswald, 48, **49**, 50, 53
Blake, Sir Francis (Crookham), 177
Blue Bell Inn, 13, 26, **27**, 65, 67,
  68, 137-8, **138**
Blue Row *see* Branxton
Branxton c/f

Branxton (cont.) *see also* wells
  Blue Row, 36, **37**, 102, **102**
  Branxton House, 11
  Branxton Villa, 36, **38**
  Flodden Crescent, 16
  memorials
    fountain, 156-7, **156**
    war memorial, 169, **169**, 170,
      170, 171
  Old Vicarage, 35, 36, **36**, 72, **72**,
    84, **84**, 91-2, **91**, 99
  plaque, village hall, 176, **176**
  St. Paul's Church, 11, 74, **75**, 81,
    85, **85**, 87, 94, **94**, 148, **148**
  Tin Tabernacle, 109-10, **109**,
    110, 124
  village, 39, 44
  Well House, 62, **62**, 127, **127**
brickwork, 21, 26, 33, 50, 64-9
  bonds, 66-7, **66**
  brick taxes, 21, 64, 66
  diapering, 67
  hand-made, 65, 132-3
  sizes, 65-6, 132
  tumbled-in, 26, 33, 67, **68**
  upright, **84**, 91
broaching, *see* droving
Butterfield, William (architect), 42
byre, 20

~

Carboniferous period, *see* geology
Carham limestone *see* geology
Carpenter, George (Ford), 183
cast iron, 119, 135-7
Cheviot *see* geology
chimney stacks c/f

chimney stacks (cont.), 113-17,
   113, **114**, **115**, **116**, **117**,
   120, **120**, 126, **126**
cornice, 113
flaunching, 113
flues, 113
parging, 114
plinth, 113
pots, 113, 117-19, **117**, **118**, **119**
shaft, 113
cills *see* windows
Clean Air Act 1956, 114
Coach House, Crookham *see*
   Crookham Cottage
coal, 1, 34, 64, 114
cob, 20, 69-70
columns, 85, **85**
corbels, 76, **76**
Corn Laws, 35
Crookham, 39, 44
   blacksmith (historic), 23-4, **24**
   Church Officer's house, 67
   Croft Gardens, 16
   Crookham Cottage, 25-6, **26**
   estate boundary wall, 146-7, **147**
   Laburnam Cottage, 106, **106**
   Manse, The, 21, **21**, 50-1, **50**, 73,
      73, 131-2, **132**
   Master's House, 36, **38**
   old dairy, 84, **84**, 139, 142, **142**
   Peace Garden, 178
   plaques
      Presbyterian School (former),
         178, **178**
      United Reformed Church, 176-
         7, **176**, **177**
   posting slot (former post office),
      143, **143**
   telephone exchange (former),
      144-5, **145**   Crookham c/f

Crookham (cont.)
   United Reformed Church, 134,
      134, 148, **148**,
   2 & 4, The Village, 22-4, **22**, **23**
   war memorials
      Crookham United Reformed
         Church, 172-3, **173**, **174**
      Crookham Village Hall, 171,
         172
   Crookham Westfield, 18-19, **18**
Culley, George, 182, **182**
Culley brothers, 35
cushion capitals, 85, **85**
   ~
Delaval (Knight) (window), 183,
   185
Delaval, Lord, 103
dentilation, 116, **116**
Devonian period *see* geology
diapering *see* brickwork
Doddington Quarry, 6
dolerite *see* geology
dolomite *see* geology
dolostones *see* geology
doors
   construction, 73-4, **73**, **74**
   furniture, 76, **76**, 138-9, **138**, **139**
   overlight, **75**
   positioning, 71-2
   style (door part), 77, **77**, 78-9, **78**
   tracery, 74, **74**
dovecote, 33
downpipes *see* roofs
dressed stone, 48, 50, **50**, 51, **51**,
   52, **52**, 56, **56**
drip moulding *see* windows
droving, 57-8, **58**, 63, **63**
drumlins *see* geology
   ~
East Barsham Manor, 64

Index

Etal *see also* wells
  Battery House, 47, **47**
  Black Bull PH, 46, **46**, 97, **98**
  Castle, 13, **14**, 27, 81
  bridge (former medieval), 164
  chantry chapel, 141
  Chapel of St. Mary, 13, 42, **43**, 44, 99, 148, **148**
  cottages (earliest), 41, **42**
  Estate (Etal only), 97
  ferry (former cable), 164
  ford, 41
  Manor, 13, **14**, 27, 36, 46, 60, 136, 152
  Manor Lodge, 125-6, **126**
  manse (former Presbyt.), 28, **28**
  mill (former), 29, **29**
  Parsonage (former), 42, **43**
  Peace Memorial Hall, 101, **101**
  plaques & memorials
    Chapel of St. Mary, 179, **179**
    building dates, 45-6
    FitzClarence/Laing, 186-7
    Peace Memorial Hall, 180, **180**
    Stone, 4th Lord Joicey, 188, **188**
  Power House, 46-7, **47**
  Presbyt. Ch (former), 13, 27-8, **28**
  village, 45, **46**
  war memorial, 174, **174**
  water spout, 141, **141**

~

fanlights *see* doors
fascia boards *see* roofs
feldspar *see* geology
fillet *see* roofs
finials *see* roofs
FitzClarence
  Augusta, Lady, 42, 179, 184
  Frederica, Lady, 179
  Frederick, Lord, 42, 179, 186-7

Flagpole Tower *see* Ford
flashing *see* roofs
flaunching *see* chimney stacks
Flodden
  battle, 28, 157-8, 178
  Brick and Tileworks, 64, 103
  ecomuseum, 178
  Memorial, 157-9, **158**
  Strip, 152
Ford *see also* wells & Waterford
  blacksmith's forge (former), 41, **41**
  Castle, 13, 36, 61, **61**, 81
  Flagpole (Cow) Tower, **12**
  game larder, 105, **105**
  King James's Tower, 82, **82**, **94**, 95
  West Lodge, 153-4, **154**
  Estate (Ford), 6, 103
  Estate (Ford & Etal), 16, 44
  Ford Church, 13, **60**, 81, **87**, 129, **129**, 136, **136**, 152, 152-3, **153**
  Jubilee Cottage, **40**, 41
  plaques & memorials
    Ford Church, 181-2, 182-3, **182**, 183-6, **185**
    Joicey & Waterford, 13, **15**
    Royal Doulton, **40**, 41
  school, 39
  war memorial, 175, **175**
  Waterford Fountain, 187, **187**
Ford Forge *see* Heatherslaw
Ford Moss colliery, 39
Ford Westfield, 89, **89**, **93**, 118
Forsyth, Rev. Moses, 177, **177**
freestone *see* sandstone

~

gabbro *see* geology
gable parapets, 67, 111, **111**, 112
  kneeler, 111, **111** gable par. c/f

209

gable parapets (cont.)
  tabling, 111, **111**
gambrel roof *see* roofs
gates (decorative), 136, **136**
gate & wall piers, 151-2, **151**, 152, **152**, 153-4, **154**, 164, **164**
geology
  andesite, 2, 7
  Avalonia, 2
  Ballagan
    Formation, 1, 4, 5
    Glen, 1
  basalt, 2
  Carboniferous period, 1,4
  Carham limestone, 5, 163
  Cheviot Massif, 1, 4
    Dyke-swarm, 2, 4
    Granite Pluton, 2, 4, 7
    Volcanic Formation, 1, 4, 7
  Devonian period, 1, 4
  dolerite, 1, 2
  dolomite, 5
  dolostones, 5
  drumlins, megadrumlins, 4
  feldspar, 7
  gabbro, 2
  granite, 2, 4
  Great Whin Sill, 1, 4, 8
  Iapetus Ocean, Suture, 2
  Ice Age, 2
  igneous rock, 1, 2, 7, **7**, 8
  Laurentia, 2
  limestone, 1, 4, 5, 64
  mica, 7
  plutonic rock, 1,2
  quartz, 7
  Quarternary period, 2, 4
  sandstone, 1, 5, **6**, 33, 39, 48, **49**, 85, 125, **125**
    fell sandstone, 1, 6 geology c/f

geology, sandstone (cont.)
  freestone, 5
  red sandstone, 85
  sedimentary rock, 1, 48
  siltstone, 1
  whinstone, 8, **8**, 9, 33, 62, **62**
Glasgow, 4th Earl of, 184
glass, 88-9, 133
granite *see* geology
Gothic style, 44, 86, **86,** 87, **87,** 94, 95
Great Whin Sill *see* geology
Grey, James (Kimmerston), 182-3
Grey, Sybil, 160
gutters *see* roofs

~

Hall, Rev. William (N. Instructor), 174, **174**
Hampton Court Palace, 64
Heatherslaw, 29-30, 33
  cottages, 123, **123**, 124
  Ford Forge, 30, **32**, 124
  Light Railway, 30
  Mill, 30, **31**, **32**, 104-5, **104**, 124
hopper heads *see* roofs
horns *see* windows
hovels, 70

~

Iapetus Ocean, Suture *see* geology
Ice Age *see* geology
igneous rock *see* geology
Industrial Revolution, 34

~

Jacobean style, 74
Jacobethan style, 131
Joicey
  1st Baron, 6, 39, 45, 97, 154
  2nd Baron, 46
  3rd Baron, 46, 180, **180**
  4th Baron, 183-4, **183**, 188, **188**

210

Index

Joicey (cont.)
  5th Baron *see* Foreword &
    Acknowledgments
  Elizabeth, Lady, 183
  Lt. Hon. D. H., 174
  plaques (house), 13, **15**
Jones, Rev. Robert (Branxton), 158
Jordan, Dorothea, 179

~

keystones *see* arches
King James's Tower *see* Ford
King's Stone, 162-4, **163**
King William IV, 179
kneeler *see* gable parapets

~

Laing, Sir James (Etal), 186-7
lancet *see* windows
Laurentia *see* geology
ledged and braced *see* doors
letter boxes, 143-4, **143**, **144**
lime mortar *see* mortar
limestone *see* geology
lime kilns, 64
lintels, 69, **69**, 79, **79**, 82, 90, **90**,
  91, 92, **92**
longhouse (style), 20

~

mansard *see* roofs
Mardon
  farm, 79-80, **79**
  farmhouse, 19, **19**, **71**, 72
margins (stonework), 63, **63**
Master's House *see* Crookham
memorials, war memorials *see*
  Branxton, Crookham, Etal, Ford
menhir, 162
Methodists, Primitive Method., 109
mica *see* geology
milemarkers, 165-8, **168**
mileposts, 165-7, **166**, **167**

Milfield Plain, 5
Mitchell, Major Charles (Pall.)
  74, 121, 139
mortar, 9, 54
  cement, 55-6, 59, 92, **92**
  deceit, 52
  joints, 51, **51**
  lime, 8, 51, 55-6, **56**, 64, 132, **132**
  pointing
    ribbon, 56, **56**
    strap, 56-7
    tuck, 52
mounting block & steps
  152-3, **153**
mullions *see* windows
muntins *see* doors & windows

~

Neville, Rev. Hastings (Ford), 149,
  150
New Etal, 41, 46

~

Old Vicarage *see* Branxton
overlight *see* doors

~

Pallinsburn, 131, 139, **139**
  Apple Store, 24-5, **25**, 65
  East Lodge, 15-16, **17**
  estate boundary wall,
    see Crookham
  gates, 136, **136**
  House, 11, **12**, 36, 50, 65, **65**, 74,
    75, 99, 121, **121**, **127**, 128, 131,
    139, **139**
  Joiner's Shop, 25, 67, **68**
  Jubilee Cottages, 69, **69**
panelled doors *see* doors
  construction
pantiles *see* tiles
parging *see* chimney stacks
parish (structure), 10

pebble-dash, 146
piers *see* gates and wall piers
pig stys, 149-50, **150**
pinnings, 58, **59**
Piper's Hill, 158
plaques
　house *see* Joicey & Waterford
　information, dedication *see* Branxton, Crookham, Etal, Ford
plutonic rock *see* geology
PVC, uPVC, 73, 119

~

quartz *see* geology
Quaternary period *see* geology
quoins, 9, 52, **52**, 53, **56**, 60, 61, **61**, 62, **62**, 63, 69, **69**, 76, **76**, 111, **111**, 120, 126, **126**, 131-2

~

railings, 136-7, **136**, **137**
rails (doors) *see* doors construction
Reavell, George (architect), 157
rebates *see* windows
rendering, 145-6
reveals *see* windows
Robertson, Sarah Askew, 157
Robertson, Watson Askew, 156, 157
Romanesque (style), 74, **85**, 94-5, **94**
roofs *see also* chimney stacks, *see also* slates, tiles
　barge boards, 124
　billet frieze, 125, **125**
　corrug. asbestos, 106, **106**, 133
　corrug. iron, 107-10, **108**, **109** **110**, 111, 133
　dormer, 102, 116, **116**, 122, **122**, **123**
　downpipes, 119-20, **120**, 121, c/f

roofs, downpipes (cont.)
　122-3, **122**, 133
　fascia boards, 120, **120**
　fillet, 112, **112**, 115, **115**, **127**
　finials, 102, 111, **112**, 116, **116**
　flashing, 102, 112, **112**, 121
　flat, 127, **127**
　gable (type), 123, **123**
　gambrel, 128-9, **129**
　　Dutch gambrel, 129, **129**
　gutters, 119-20, **120**, 121, 122-3, **122**, **123**, 133
　hipped (type), 125-6, **126**
　hopper heads, 119-20, 121, **121**, 133, 138, **138**
　mansard (type), 128, **128**
　porch, 102, **102**
　shed (type), 127, **127**
　thatch, 20, 22, **23**, **24**, 25, 46, 96, 97, **98**, 133
roughcast, 146
rubble
　random, 9, 22, 27-8, 33, 48, 53, 55, 56, **57**, 61-2, 92, **92**
　built to courses, 53, **54**, 81, **81**
　squared, 120
rustication, 59-60, **60**
rybats, 62-3, **63**, 69, **69**, 82, 90, **90**, 92

~

sandstone *see* geology
Sandyford Farm, 81, **81**, 92, **92**
sarking *see* slates
sedimentary rock *see* geology
siltstone *see* geology
slates, 21, 96
　graduated, 101, **101**
　Lakeland, 99
　nailing, 100-1
　patterned, **100**　　　　slates c/f

Index

slates (cont.)
  sarking, 100-1
  Scottish, 99, **99**, 101
  slabs, 102
  Spanish, 99-100
  Welsh, 99, 102, 116, **116**, 120, **120**
  Westmorland, 99
snecks, 59, **59**
Solway Plain, 20
spalling, 55
squared rubble *see* rubble
stiles (door) *see* doors construction
stugging, 57-8, **58**, **59**, 62, **63**, 132, **132**
Sutherland, Sir Arthur, 177

~

tabling *see* gable parapets
telephone boxes, 142-3, **142**
thatch *see* roofs
tiles
  asbestos cement, 106-7, **106**
  clay, 96
  concrete, 104, 105, **105**, 120, **120**
  fish scale, 105, **105**
  pantiles, 102-5, **103**, **104**
  ridge, 102, **102**, 116, **116**
  Roman, 105
  torching, 103, 105
township (structure), 10
tracery *see* doors and windows
trades, 10-11, **11**
transom *see* windows
transportation (improved), 26, 64
tuck pointing *see* mortar
Tudor style, 44
Tweed basin, 5

~

United Ref. Church *see* Crookham
uPVC *see* PVC

~

Venetian windows, 24-5, 67, **68**
vermiculation, 61, **61**
vernacular style, 46

~

Waterford
  Lady Waterford Hall, 13, 39, **40**, 76, **76**, **100**, 105, 124
  Louisa, Lady, 6, 39, 76, 124, 160, 185-6, 187
  plaques (house), 13, **15**, 153
  3rd Marquess, 39, 187, **187**
water pillars, 140, **140**, **141**
wells
  Branxton (Marmion's, Sybil's) 160, **161**, 162
  Ford, 140, **141**
  Marmion's (Sybil's, Flodden Hill), 159-60, **159**
  site of St. Mary's chantry chapel, Etal, 141
whinsill *see* Great Whinsill
whinstone *see* geology
Williams, Capt. Theodore (ADC-Lord FitzClarence), 179
windows
  agricultural, 91-2, **91**, **92**
  arrow slit, 82, **82**
  bay, 126, **126**, 133
  casement, 83, 90
  cills, 69, **69**, 82, 90, **90**, 92, **92**
  Crittall, 90-1, **91**
  drip moulding, 85, **85**, 86-7, **86** **87**, **87**
  history, 81-3
  horns, 84
  mullions, 82, **82**, 85, **85**
  muntins, 83, **83**, 84, **84**, 90, **90**
  positioning, 71-2
  rebates, 86   windows c/f

213

windows (cont.)
　reveals, 86
　sash, 82-4, **83**, **84**, 85, **85**, 89, **89**
　stop ends, 87, **87**
　tracery, 74, 82, **94**, 95
　transom, 83
　trefoil, 95
　workshop, 89-90, **90**, 90-1, **91**
wrought iron, 135-9